JUMEIRAH

AL SATWA

DUBAI
CREEK

DEIRA

BURJ
KHALIFA

BUSINESS BAY

BUR DUBAI

DUBAI
INTERNATIONAL
AIRPORT

UNCOMMON
DUBAI

EDITED BY HIND SHOUFANI

Published by Uncommon Ltd.

ISBN 9789995706081
Printed in Italy

The opinions expressed in this book are those of the authors etc.
Facts are deemed correct at time of going to print,
some may be subject to change.

Managing Editor Dora Bouhara
Executive Editor Emma Mattei
Design Jon Banthorpe
Stock Photography:
Mohamad Badr p.13
Basile Mookherjee p.127
Lamya Gargash p.226-7

Uncommon Ltd.
168 St. Christopher Street
VLT 1476
Valletta, Malta.
www.uncommonguidebooks.com

"As you draw near to the land / at night keep distance, lest you encounter reefs,
And if you are sailing on a big ship / be vigilant and display your courage."

Ahmad ibn Majid

INDEX

REFLECTION, DUBAI MARINA

FOREWORD

Dubai's development, at the centre of the exponentially spinning growth rate of the Arabian Gulf region, might be termed explosive by some.

Between 1968 and 1975, Dubai's population grew by over three hundred per cent. With eighty-seven per cent of its population foreign born, Dubai makes many of the multicultural cities of the West look demographically homogenous.

Located on the Emirates' Northern coastline, Dubai now has a skyline that is world famous in its infancy.

Dubai's history boasts a kaleidoscope of people: bedouins and farmers, migrant cultures and a dynamic Western expat base that live in a skyscraper and highway metropolis, all mingling with the local Emirati city-dweller culture.

Touted 'World Winning City' in 2002, the city's population doubled between 2002 and 2008 to now have the largest population in the UAE, at 2.1 million residents, in the second-largest land territory, 4,114 km^2, after the capital Abu Dhabi. In 2008, Dubai experienced as much property development as Shanghai, a city with thirteen times its population.

This boom began in the early 1980s with the re-energising of the under-utilised Jebel Ali Port, declaring it Dubai's first Free Zone. It flourished and became one of the busiest ports in the world. Today, it processes over ten million shipping containers annually, and now there are many Free Zones in Dubai, where business is rampant.

Its lack of sustainable oil production has caused Dubai to style itself - in dramatic super-star overnight fashion - into a commerce, trade and real estate hub, as well as a prominent leisure destination, voicing louder thoughts than its sibling emirates, or other Gulf cities nearby.

Bur Dubai, the historically older district of Dubai, translates to *Mainland Dubai* -referencing the age-old separation of the Bur Dubai area from Deira by the water. The Dubai creek is a joyful discovery to many visitors who cross it in small, hired wooden *Abra*, to find respite from the lavishness of 'New Dubai'.

As the prime secure destination for people in the tumultuous Middle Eastern region, and a hub for international seasoned business and leisure travellers transcending East and West, Dubai's marvel - an amalgam of extraordinary architecture, spatial development and bigger construction sites - has been lambasted, as well as applauded, in media outlets and living rooms, simultaneously smeared and revered in countless publications and bars alike.

In this guidebook we delve into the dichotomy of Dubai, between those who admire and invest in the city and those who feel unsettled by its novelty. We approach the stories of people as avenues to the city's unfolding map, and where there are people, there is culture to be made.

Uncommon: Dubai is a counterpoint to ubiquitous travel guides and saccharine tourist recommendations. Here is an intimate companion that can deftly guide you through the veneer and into the well-worn streets of our city, taking you on a journey that hopes for unexpected encounters for the curious senses.

HIND SHOUFANI   2014

RELATE

OUR ELDERS ARE A BLESSING

TEXT + PHOTOGRAPHY: **LAMYA GARGASH**

Space plays a big role in my society. It's a crucial element in our social agenda, where we sit or gather around to converse and interact.

Family values are important and making sure that these ties are secure is essential in most Middle Eastern & Arab families.

With my family, prior to the death of my grandmother, Friday mornings and afternoons (sometimes they would bleed into the early evenings) would be family day at my grandmother's. She lived with my aunt and uncle. The house would be filled with lots and lots of people - aunts, uncles, cousins, nannies, friends and babies. It's hard not to get lost in all this noise and clutter. People on their phones, talking, eating, watching TV, some even attempting to read a book or a journal, kids playing in the background and always so much food to go around. The hard part is trying to find your shoes when you decide to leave or move this social scenario into the garden. There are hundreds of shoes, sandals, slippers laid at the entrance of the living room. I always made sure to lay my shoes behind the plant pot, ensuring no one would move them, or decide to borrow them for the day.

Socialising didn't just take place in the living room, it also took place in the bedrooms. My grandmother would be on her bed and everyone would be around her, with my aunt at one end, laying out her prayer matt on the floor as she fixed her praying veil. On the adjacent sofa another aunt, laying out her nail polish bottles and deciding which colour to paint her nails, many of us sitting on the floor with our teacups and snacks on the tiny coffee table, some of us checking our phones, others involved in dramatic conversations. One word can be used to describe this scene - vibrant.

The TV was most definitely on, to add more drama to an already intense setting. This scene was not limited to females only, as male family members would pop in to pay respects to my grandmother. They would approach her bed, slip in a kiss on the head or hand.

My father's side of the family is much smaller than that of my mother's. My grandfather was one of three boys but had many half sisters. Growing up I have a vague memory of my great aunts visiting my grandmother and my great grandmother (their step mother). They would come in the afternoons and sit on a porch-like setting that was in close proximity to my great grandmother's room and was an extension of the living room. They would watch us play outdoors on our bikes and roller skates. The ground was not smooth at all; it was once a garden but my grandmother decided that plants were too bothersome and had them removed, and this Eden of a garden was replaced with this horrible concrete flooring that gave the courtyard a very barren look.

My mother tried very hard to make our house and garden a home, we lived in the same compound, filled with plant pots and swings and slides. It was important that we spent as much time as possible outdoors , so with a little imagination, it never really bothered us that the floor was uneven and full of stones.

My grandmother only bore my grandfather two sons, my father and his brother. So visiting my father's side of the family was not as crazy, but still fairly intense. Respecting the elders is crucial, and these family reunions attempt to formalise them.

Weekends in the past were Thursdays and Fridays, and then the weekend was changed to Friday and Saturday. So our Thursday family visit had inevitably changed to Saturdays (Fridays were dedicated to my mother's side of the family). Since my immediate paternal side of the family is small, we had many of our extended relatives pop in for visits. My father's family had moved around quite a bit before settling into their current and present home. When my father had informed me that my great grandfather's house was still standing, I knew that one day I would pay that house a visit, intrigued by history and wanting to understand and see where my grandfather grew up. There had always been this internal drive to visually preserve what remains of this personal infrastructure.

It was a compound and though my great grandfather owned it, many other family members lived there, and in its day (more than a 120 years ago) it was considered one of the biggest houses.

I did eventually go and seek the place out for myself. Unfortunately the doors had been auctioned off, and now they sit in my uncle's *Majlis*, the formal sitting area. So I did not get the whole experience I envisioned as I entered the space, but I sought to make the best of it anyway. Another family lives there now, and they have attempted to make it their own. Many questions lurked in my head as to why this beautiful, old house, probably one of the very few remaining houses of its kind in the country, is falling apart with no care to preserve it. The question was easy but the answer was not.

After the death of my great grandfather the house was to be divided amongst many. As the family grew, and with the years speeding by, the situation got more intense and complex. Approval from hundreds of members was required before anything could be done to attempt to hold it up and fix it, and with everyone completely immersed in their own lives, no one would to take it upon him or herself to take on this challenge.

I walked on the same grounds that many of my ancestors and family members have walked on. I wondered, what conversations took place there? What emotions ran through? Waking up every morning and experiencing each day, how did that take place? Humans surrender to their mortality with only buildings, spaces and infrastructures to remind us of the frailty of life, to remind us of the lives that occurred within them as well.

So here it is this beautiful historical landmark surrendering. Bit by bit, the house falls. The new residents trying their best to familiarise the space, setting up satellite dishes to ease their lifestyle.

Roaming around the rooms, it was hard to foresee myself stepping into the past because of all these modern intrusions. A relative was with me and she cried. It hit hard. The past is gone. Family too will be forgotten. These spaces, young and old, remind us of days filled with tears and joy. One breath overlapping the other, human existence all around, reflected in spaces that once captured them.

FATA MORGANA

PHOTOGRAPHY: **BALAZS GARDI**

DUBAI, DECONSTRUCTED

TEXT + PHOTOGRAPHY: **ROBERT FERRY**

We arrived in Dubai exactly one month before the Lehman Brothers collapse shockwave left downtown Manhattan. It was just enough of a head start that I was able to talk to a job recruiter while the construction boom in Dubai was still humming blissfully. The recruiter and I met at Second Cup in the Mall of the Emirates and talked about prospects, while skiers enjoyed the nearby slopes despite the 48°C temperature outside.

The Mall was a convenient 10-minute walk to our new apartment, Summerland Al Barsha. We were the first people to move in there and so we did double duty as tenant and punch-list reviewer. Over the course of our four years in Dubai, we would live in three different apartments - Al Barsha, Bur Dubai, and Dubai Marina - the last of which was the most glamorous (a newer Emaar property called Park Island, which if you look closely enough you'll find an exact replica of downtown, across from the Burj Khalifa).

The meeting with the recruiter that day landed me a job working in Masdar City, Abu Dhabi, during the early days when the plan was still to make a net-zero carbon city for 40,000 inhabitants. It was an incredibly unique experience, an education like none other, and it introduced me to the complicated interrelationship between the ambitions of sustainability and the harsh realities of the UAE climate, lack of potable water and subsidised energy costs.

The idea of Dubai is rooted in the imagination of its rulers; it is also a beacon to the world, enticing wealthy tourists and foreign capital, in order to build a self-perpetuating economy based on industry, trade and commerce, rather than on oil. On the surface Dubai is an impressive success, however the speed at which the city was built has not allowed for a comprehensive integration of sustainable infrastructures. The development arms race created when Nakheel, Emaar, and Dubai Holding were set up to compete against each other did not result in a centralised set of building or zoning codes.

The result was on display when we arrived at the Cityscape Real Estate Exhibition at the Dubai World Trade Centre in September, 2008. Nakheel was there to unveil their Nakheel Harbour and Tower; planned at over 1,000 metres it would have exceeded the height of the Burj Khalifa by at least 25%. But today Emaar is still in the lead as it soon became clear that Nakheel would have to scrap those plans (and its plans for the Dubai Waterfront, etc.) once the world financial crisis finally hit Dubai's markets. Standing today at the base of the Burj Khalifa, it is almost unimaginable that a free-standing tower could ever be 25% taller. As powerful as that view is from the Dubai Mall walk up to the top of the Burj Khalifa, and as impressive as the canyon of commerce is to drive through along Shekh Zayed Road financial centre, perhaps the most humbling pedestrian view is to stand in the alleyways of the mega-block adjacent to Dubai Marina (look for Ocean Heights, Marina 101 and the Marina Crown) where there are ten buildings taller than the Empire State building, so close together that you could toss a ball between them.

While visiting the city it is interesting to notice which of the three developers' properties you find yourself walking within because you will notice some commonalities. Nakheel typically has the waterfront and land reclamations (the Palm and the World projects), and also has the Jumeirah Lake Towers, Ibn Battuta Mall, Dragon Mart (if

you have a full week, this is worth seeing - it looks like a dragon from space!), International City, The Gardens and Discovery Gardens. Emaar has the Downtown with the Dubai Mall and the Burj Khalifa, and also the beautiful Dubai Marina. Dubai Holding has the Jumeriah Group Hotels (Burj al Arab and Madinat Jumeirah), Business Bay, TECOM, the Jumeirah Beach Residence (JBR), JBR Walk, and a lot of the things that end in 'City' (Knowledge City, Media City, Internet City, Healthcare City, etc.).

Dubai takes as its point of departure the idea of the future as it was understood at the middle of the 20th century. Dubai's glass skyscrapers are inspired by the mind of F.T. Marinetti by way of 20th century New York City, Vancouver, Singapore and other more temperate and tropical climates but there has been inconsistent regard for what it means to construct buildings on a desert coast - such a delicate and complicated ecosystem. The notion of the superlative, for which Dubai has excelled, has so far not translated into a regard for superlative sustainable models of development. There have been some efforts, especially Dubai Electricity and Water Authority (DEWA) that has been easing back from energy and water subsidies, and continues to update its Green Building Regulations, and it is no longer possible to construct a building that is an environmental disaster.

If you want to learn more about Dubai's potential to become sustainable, you must visit The Change Initiative (TCI) on Sheikh Zayed Road near the Ibis Al Barsha. The contemporary buildings that have given a nod to sustainable design over the past decade, such as The Index and O-14, are drawing on the passive design lessons from the past. And to learn about how the city functioned in the days before fossil-fuel-powered air conditioning, all you have to do is spend a couple of days between Bur Dubai and Deira.

While on the Bur Dubai side of the creek, our favourite walk was to start in Al Fahedi and make our way by back streets to Al Bastakiya through all of the fabric traders and restaurants. Spend some time in Bastakiya. While all of the *barjeel*[1] towers are now only ornamental, you can still get a sense from the architecture how the thick gypsum and coral walls, the areesh (palm frond) walls and ceiling that allowed for air circulation, and the courtyards and alleys oriented to capture prevailing winds, all worked together to passively create more comfortable living environments despite the extreme heat of the climate. Leaving Bastakiya, take a left at the creek and walk along the water until the plaza opens up after the Ruler's Court (mind the pigeons). There you will get lost in the charming alleyways surrounding the Hindu Temple. The main lane there will lead you out into the crowds of the Old Souk, but don't miss the blue-tiled Iranian Mosque which you can get to by diving back into the neighbourhood away from the creek.

While you are in this part of Bur Dubai (and also while in Deira and Satwa), pay attention to the architecture from the late 60s - Dubai's first-wave postmodern architecture, which just slightly predates the effect of nearly free energy on the architecture. Some of these buildings are marked by lower floor-to-floor heights, smaller windows, and by mid-century modern variations on *mashrabiya*[2] and on the cornice expression of the barjeel. The most prominent within this classification is of course the World Trade Centre. While visiting, don't miss seeing the powerful axis that frames this classic as seen from the DIFC Gate and through the very stately Emirates Towers.

Following the water again past the Abra station and the bend in the creek, you can finish your Bur Dubai adventure with some time

1. ARCHITECTURAL ELEMENT TO CREATE VENTILATION.

2. A BAY WINDOW ENCLOSED WITH CARVED WOOD LATTICEWORK.

in Shindagha, where you will find the 1896 built home of Sheikh Saeed Al Maktoum and the 1928 home of Sheikh Jumaa al Maktoum. Both residences now house museums, the latter being the House of Traditional Architecture, which is a not-to-miss exhibit that will teach you everything you could want to know about the historic architecture, construction details, and urban planning of Dubai. If you want a change from the charming but diesel-smelling abras, you can always take the pedestrian tunnel at the end of Shindagha to cross into Deira, where a visit to the Al-Ahmadiya School and Heritage House is another must-see traditional gem - a peek into the pearl-diving history of the city.

For a look at the vernacular architecture of the present it is interesting to take a stroll through the single family residential developments of Al Barsha 2 behind the Mall of the Emirates - a great example of the Dubai version of the North American McMansion phenomenon. Over the past decade there has emerged a new style throughout the Gulf region that has some consistencies, characterised by a large cornice and columns that terminate into the underside of the soffit without entablature, as well as double-story porte-cocheres, gregarious double-staired entry foyers and large garages.

Stop at the Dubai Mall metro station, but instead of following the crowd, take a walk to the other side of Sheikh Zayed Road, where - after crossing Al Albaany Street - you'll come upon a delightfully understated little *freej* with an undeveloped park-like area behind it. There you will find graffiti walls that speak of the tenuous nature of their neighbourhood—waiting for the future and reminded of changes by the ever-present Burj.

RECOMMENDED READING: *A HISTORY OF FUTURE CITIES* BY DANIEL BROOK (W. W. NORTON & COMPANY, 2013).

BEST VIEW: FROM THE ROOF LEVEL OF THE BANIYAS STREET PARKING GARAGE NEAR THE SPICE SOUK IN DEIRA.

MOST INTERESTING MOSQUE: FUTTAIM MASJID ON MAKTOUM HOSPITAL ROAD IN DEIRA JUST OFF AL SABKHA ROAD (A RARE AND SUCCESSFUL USE OF RED BRICK IN DUBAI ARCHITECTURE).

BEST OUTDOOR DINING: BLUE BARJEEL ALONG DUBAI CREEK.

BEST LOCAL (INEXPENSIVE) BAR: THE COWBOYS IN THE PRESIDENT HOTEL NEAR THE AL KARAMA METRO STOP.

ODDEST SIGHT: THE VILLA THAT WAS RECENTLY BUILT ALONG THE JUMEIRAH 1 PUBLIC BEACH. DRAW A STRAIGHT LINE ON A MAP FROM THE BURJ KHALIFA TO THE BEACH AND YOU'LL SEE IT ON GOOGLE EARTH. IT'S THE THING THAT LOOKS LIKE A SPACESHIP.

WHO REMEMBERS AMNESIA?

TEXT: **AUSTYN ALLISON**

PHOTOGRAPHY: **AUSTYN ALLISON + FIONA PATTERSON**

Old-timers in Dubai love to talk about what the city was like when they got here, what has now vanished and what has arrived. There were never fields and trees to mourn, but there's the buildings.

After eight years I'm an old-timer by Dubai standards. I was here before Mall of the Emirates. I was here before Ibn Battuta mall.

I watched the Burj Khalifa go up, one floor a week, and could measure how long I'd been in Dubai against its height. I would sit in the yard of the villa where I first lived, rocking on the green and white swing chair, and look over from Satwa, past the Fairmont hotel and over Sheikh Zayed Road as what would become the tallest tower in the world emerged at the illusive speed of the sun here. You can never see the movement of sun or skyscraper, but the next time you look it's moved.

And then the Burj was complete. After four years of waiting the last crane was removed. There were fireworks at the grand opening of the tallest structure ever, and I was there. Parachutes landed, speeches were made, plaques were uncovered, the name was changed and the city put the candle on the greatest cake ever created.

Then buildings in Dubai began to come down.

The Hard Rock Cafe was one of them. For those who were already veterans when I arrived, it used to be the outpost of Dubai, the sign you were leaving the city on your way to Jebel Ali and Abu Dhabi, or the mark that you were reaching civilisation again returning from the south. To me, it had been the one old sentry of Media City, a fabled land of easy visas and jet setting media jobs, further out of town in the New Dubai, far from my Satwa and from Gulf News where I flew out to work in 2005.

But it was closed in 2009 and demolished at the start of 2013. By that time I was working in Media City, and living in the Marina. I had left the low-rise, ramshackle foreign-ness of Satwa and had moved to the shiny side, where poor people are invisible and, like a college campus, the residents need never leave. Media City had grown around the Hard Rock, the Marina had grown beyond it, and it stood dwarfed but proud like a duck among swans.

Dubai writes its own history. And it erases its own history when it tires of it. It renames streets and it moves memories. Today's incarnation of the Hard Rock Cafe is in Festival City, which was just another Creek-side sandpit when I landed. People come and go so fast here that the original restaurant soon will only exist in the memories of those who no longer have ties to this place. One day I will be one of them.

Dubai isn't somewhere you think of things getting demolished; it is a place of building and architectural creation.

But landmarks - both public and personal - are demolished. The Grand Millennium hotel, home to the oldest pub in Dubai where we began Karl's stag do, was demolished in 2012, so was the Al Nasr cinema. After it had closed down, I snuck in and scrabbled about in the dark, glimmers from door cracks revealing the tatty seats, graffiti, a faded sign prohibiting tea upstairs. It was somewhere I had never been, and exploring it was like listening to the eulogy of a man you know only through the fond stories of friends. How many children had seen their first film there? How many couples held hands in the dark on awkward first dates?

One morning, as the last levels were being added to the Burj and Dubai's building bloom was blossoming, I came out of the villa in Satwa to find green numbers sprayed on the wall. My home was marked for destruction to make room for a whole new city.

When the Hard Rock Cafe was being knocked down it took months, and my Media City office overlooked it.

Despite its landmark status, the restaurant only dated back to December 1997 and Chuck Berry played a concert to inaugurate it. Sand coloured, it resembled a miniature Empire State Building with a globe at the top of its spire and giant crossed guitars in front.

I only went to the Hard Rock Cafe once, in May 2007. I'd landed a job in Media City and dragged a new colleague there for lunch on my first day. There was a '50s convertible suspended from the ceiling, hairy men in biker jackets and framed LPs on the walls.

Although music memorabilia has been the main selling point of the global Hard Rock Cafe franchise since 1971, I paid the decor little attention. If you already live in a city, you're not there to see the sights; you're there for food, drink and conversation. I assumed there would be time to take in the exhibits at leisure. There wasn't.

I wish I had explored the Hard Rock Cafe after it was abandoned, as I had the Al Nasr cinema and my villa. In there, I'd have seen if the car was still hanging from the roof. I like to think they left it there. I doubt they did, but it wasn't really rock memorabilia like Keith Richard's comb or Elvis's last cigar, and who really wants an upside-down car?

Hoardings were erected in front of the site, telling passers-by this building is old, this building is over, this building is already dead. Please move along; there is no longer anything to see.

One day a mobile crane came with a wrecking ball. It started battering the bottom of the back, the non-road side, of the Hard Rock. The 3.5-tonne pendulum swung into the wall and surprisingly little happened. Slow pieces would fall off. Persistence, rather than strength or speed or ferocity, was the essence of the assault.

For a bit of variety the crane driver sometimes raised his ball and dropped it on to the roof. Occasionally the ball would get caught.

The Hard Rock Cafe's essence was gone now and I was a disinterested observer. Panels began to peel off the tower, and there was nothing beneath. That was a disappointment. I had hoped to see at least the remains of an office in there, a single bedroom perhaps. But no one had ever looked out from those miniature Empire State windows. From the road, it was hard to see the building was dying until you could see daylight through the front door with no restaurant behind it.

Then the inevitable happened when the arm of one guitar broke. For those without an aerial office view, that was the sign it was really over. There had been a radio campaign to save the guitars. A station petitioned for them to be moved, perhaps to the gates of Studio City.

Rumour tells that the station got its way. The site's owners told the producers they could have the guitars, but they would have to transport them. Massive lumps of concrete and rebar aren't light, and the station didn't have the money, the facilities or the inclination to move them when the offer came. So it kept on calling for them to be rescued, knowing it had already turned down the guitars' last chance of salvation.

Not long after the guitars broke, the mobile crane picked up its ball and left, and a taller, fixed crane took its place. It would lower a basket and men methodically removed the superstructure. First the globe went, then the remaining panels from the tower. Then the scaffold inside. A bulldozer took care of what was left of the base.

After the machines went, the rubble was carted off, and nothing was left but sand. Now I park beside where the Hard Rock Cafe used to stand. Unless you know what was once there, it's just more sand by the side of Sheikh Zayed Road. There are new buildings that look over it from all around, and as people come to Dubai and leave, fewer and fewer who look down on the sand will remember the Hard Rock Cafe. I do, though. I remember how it was once the last outpost of an exciting city where everything was new and exciting, where anything could happen, where a newcomer could watch the world's tallest tower emerge, where, if the rumours were believed, he would one day work in Media City, and where the future would rise and the past would descend like the sun.

AND DEEP OUR HYBRID ROOTS LIE

TEXT: **JAMAL IQBAL**

IMAGE: **ANOUSHKA ANAND**

"Why was he speaking with me in Hindi? I can speak English fluently, and made sure I answered him in English only."

I remember my mother telling me this, rather peeved, a few years ago, as she described her first pass via Dubai customs. I wished to explain to her that his attempts at English were not a sign of him doubting her knowledge of the language. In fact, they were probably a sign of the young Emirati's hospitality, a need to show off his knowledge of an alien culture he had grown up with, was fascinated by and still curious about. A constant fugue state he found himself living in. Caused by the sensorial surplus that pockets of the Asian community brought with them to this young city.

I didn't tell her. I also didn't tell her that Dubai was more home to me now, than India ever was. Fact is, when I first chose Dubai over Mombasa, I didn't know that myself either.

It's quite easy to understand the appeal this city holds for us from the sub-continent. If I were to explain it to you using my own little supposition, it's to do with our senses – all seven of them. The five

you are conventionally aware of. The sixth, a spirituality that *desis*[1] inherit in utero. And the seventh, a capitalistic fervour my generation inherently grows to worship, even as we cling on to our Gods. *Our* personal fugue, as we try and balance complex subtleties much like the spices we marinate with, the emotions in our cinema and the metaphors in our literature.

Walk the *desi* streets and you will find shards of sound, breathe in frankincense and spice, stare at vivid vibrance, get jostled ever so gently and taste the most eclectic and complex, sometimes all at once. I'm often asked why we are so darned loud. But when you come from countries where a billion of you eke out a zombiesque existence that for most part doesn't even guarantee you a tenth of the social security 'the first world' offers, loud is just a means to express individualism. Even as we go about creating our own little world, confirming to the rules and idioms of life as expatriates.

To discover this unique hybrid, go to the areas on the other side of the creek if you must. But prior to diving into those labyrinthine lanes, walk down Oud Metha Street to Lamcy Plaza. Where on the 2nd of every month, you will find the Al Ansari Exchange thronging with Indians and Pakistanis, remitting money home. The reason they live in the city, sometimes all alone, at times in plush apartments, others seven to a room? The exchange rate! Should the Wall Street crash, and the dollar go less bullish on the rupee – you will see the exchange deserted, until a string of text messages goes from smartphone to smartphone - "*Rupiya baitha hua hai, aaj bhej*" (The Rupee is down, send today).

Outside the plaza to the right is Lamcy Cinema, probably the only cinema in the world sold out on Thursday 2.00 am screenings! A

1. A TERM FOR THE PEOPLE AND CULTURE OF THE INDIAN SUBCONTINENT OR SOUTH ASIA AND FOR THEIR DIASPORA.

Thursday viewing gets you bragging rights of having been to the *First Day First Show* of Indian blockbusters (released in the UAE every Thursday, as opposed to India's Friday releases). To all *desis*, the First Day First Show or the FDFS phenomenon is sacred. Even more so if you happen to be a film buff, an actor or an aspiring one - all rolled into one in most cases. FDFS lets you be the first to post 'Saw DDLJ FDFS and it was total PV'! (I saw *Dilwale Dulhaniya Le Jayenge* First Day First Show and it was completely *paisa vasool*, value for money.) Movies are savoured with *Samosas* – a snack we claim as our own, one that ironically originated as the Middle Eastern *Sambousek*. And *b*awling babies are par for the course - Bollywood starts early when you're a *desi*! There is an 'interval' in the middle, just as the plot finally brews, for you to rush for a smoke, or more samosas. And as soon as the words 'The End' appear on screen, there's a hustle to leave the theatre, credit roll be damned. A Pavlovian leftover from the rush to beat crowded streets and even more crowded bylanes back home.

The bylanes outside Lamcy Plaza though, are a *desi* gourmand's delight, offering flavours from every part of the subcontinent. Where the food, the ambience and the service will be colourful, chaotic and quite nonchalant when it comes to time - IST standing for Indian Stretchable Time. It's also likely that at most Indian eateries you will be asked for change, so drilled are the traditional 'coin shortage, tender exact change' socialist days from the 80s. So do keep small bills handy.

Start with the *Shabri nihari*, a secret slow cooked curry served with foot-long *nans* at the B&B Cricket Café (owned by Pakistani cricketers). Or hop across to Punjabi by Nature (authentically pronounced *punjabbbi bie naitturr*) for *Arbi* (yam) *tikkas*, *makki* (corn) *roti* and *Amritsari macchi* (mustard fish) washed down with *aam panna*, a roasted mango and pepper drink.

The food trail continues with Sai Dham, its *satvik* Indian food bereft of supposed libido enhancers like onion and garlic, served on copper plates as prayer *bhajans* play in the background. Then, if you wish to indulge a sweet tooth, walk a block further to the Haji Ali juice centre, with its iconic mango and *sitaphal* (custard apple), cream desserts, and *Billo* ice cream right across from it – an uber-kitschy joint with Pakistani truck art as its livery. If you can spot the Indian and the Pakistani flags on the kitsch-art replica of the Delhi Red Fort, you'll realise that the co-existence of India and Pakistan in Dubai is quite a contrast to the decades-long jingoistic hate rhetoric that plays out between these two countries back home, blaring on national news, played out on cricket fields and reaching its nadir at the yearly gun battles we fight with toyed soldiers on the Kashmir border every year when the snow melts. In Dubai though, we're BFFs, still in slight awe of the Caucasians and refusing, for the most part, to even attempt to learn Arabic. An *amused bouche*, for cynics like me as I watch us tucking into *pani puris* by the dozen at *Chatori Galli*, just outside Oud Metha station.

The ritual of the perfect custom created *pani puri* is an intricate exercise in timing and balance of flavours. It starts with choosing the right *puri* fritter, semolina or wheat. You then choose the stuffing, generally boiled, spiced potato for North Indians and Pakistanis, a dash of onion for the Bengalis and sprouts for the Bombay crowd. Once selected, the *puri* maker adds a dash of spice and carefully balances out portions of chilled water, one sweet, one tangy that your *puri* gets dunked into by turn and pop - it goes into your bowl and to your mouth. Once you're satiated, you hold a bowl out for extra water, which you drink straight out of the bowl and, as duly trained, you ask for a *suukka* when done. A freebie fritter with a mix of dry, spice powders.

In fact it's the 'extra' that sets you out as a regular. A quirk, that carries itself into almost every *desi* transaction, from the extra *sambar* you will ask for at any South Indian *idli* restaurant, to the traditional *champi*, a free massage you get at the end of any visit to the desi 'hair cutting salon'. Replete with the barber's penchant for applying matchsticks on shaving nicks and insisting on inserting his thumbs into your ear as the *champi* goes on.

For more sensorial quirks, make your way one evening to the Al Fahidi Street Historical District, known colloquially as Mina Bazaar. Bargain with the chap selling you fake Rolex watches, and you'll soon realise there are genuine fakes and cheap fakes! Walk the bustling blocks and you might run into Sejal, who speaks seven languages and Fakih who claims to speak eighteen, all in the hope of not disappointing the right tourist. Take a peek into Sheeba and see for yourself how the smells of Versace and Armani and YSL coexist with the traditional *Kurtas* and silk dresses of Ayappa's next door. In fact Al Fahidi street is a delight to the eyes, with textiles ranging from South Indian *Tussar* Silk to the ubiquitous *Pashmina* jostling for space with Pakinstani *Zardozy*, Bengali *Katha* and Lucknowi *Chikankari* dresses, all rounded up by Parmar Tailors – giving you a bespoke suit that's on par with the best Seville Row has to offer – the cutters on both streets hail from Lucknow, the same part of India. Or so the legend goes.

And in this hub of commerce you will run into the colourful Mehfil 1, at the Royal Ascot Hotel. A themed bar where Bollywood dreams come crashing amidst a grunge filled assault of bustiers and *ghagras*, as young Indian and Nepalese girls gyrate for your voyeuristic pleasure, night after night. On a ramp that's a hundred metres long, replete with little people, emcees and cheap Chinese strobe lights. Where tips of a few thousand dirhams are par for the course, as are gold necklaces, amorous or otherwise. A parallel economy, just a block away from Temple Street, where coconuts are broken and the Goddess garlanded even as married men end their quest for glitz over chilled beer. What sets Mehfil 1 apart – I've seen entire families, wife, kids et al, enjoying the show. It's quite, PG13.

But as I said before, amidst the loud cacophony of commerce the *desi* constantly seeks to appease his roots. The fugue state resurfaces as *Gulfis* (2nd generation Indians and Pakistani kids in Dubai) with their skinny jeans and styled spikes will ever so often be found learning *Carnatic* music at the Crystal Shruthi Institute, and *Hindustani* classical music and dance at the Ajivasan Gurukul just above Al Adil grocery in Karama. Ostensibly, far, far away from 'bad influence'! Pop by and listen to them practice their *ragas*. Then step into Al Adil with its traditional flour-mill and an instant lesson in how the *Bombay Mix* actually comes in with at least fifty variations, (including *diet chewdas*) all suited to taste. The same *Gulfis* shall then smoke shishas and party at *desi* ladies' nights at 'Noir by Pulse' every Tuesday, twirling to *Yo Yo Honey Singh's* 'bhangrap' while their parents visit Ayeda Hussain's monthly Sufi Meditations, in an area quite sardonically named Poppy Lane, the Green Community.

Ayeda is a journalist, a charming, witty conversationalist and someone who converts her prayer room into a wonderful meditation spot once a month. She brings with her a sense of calm that ever so often succeeds in delineating the light, within the complexity that is the *desi*'s Dubai.

A city that for me is part desert, part steel and all seven senses; a city where I recreated myself physically and artistically; a city for the perpetual seeker; a city where, once I began seeing through the branded handbags, the fast cars and the glitter, I found a melancholia only the lonely traveller can see. Someone that knows that home here is permanent impermanence.

He touches down the walkway to dreamland.
Smells good, he says.
Shadows of those he left.
Still visible, he says.
Scar tissue, formed over an alien land living a stowaway's days.
There's always a balm, he says.
Manna, served in capitalistic upsize.
Tastes good, he says.
A billion tongues, entwine with the sound of his pidgin voice.
Sounds great, he says.
Each swipe of his Platinum plus adds another $\sqrt{}$ to the anti-bucket list.
Clink on, he says.
Atheist, don't you worship any more?
Karma, he says.

THE DELIRIOUS TYPOGRAPHIC CITY

TEXT: HUDA SMITSHUIJZEN ABIFARES

The energy of a city, and certainly one as 21st-century as Dubai, can best be measured by the writing on its walls. I am not talking here about literal writing on the walls, as in urban graffiti, but about the kind of ubiquitous writing that matches the energy of its urban host; one that shapes and guides its daily activities; text that visually defines the city's character through urban signs, advertising, newspapers and magazines. So what would a 'Dubai type' look like? The question is simple but the answer is not.

Let me first describe what *type* of city Dubai is. I ask myself this as I sit here behind my laptop on the 22nd floor of a 41-storey building, in a part of the city filled with high-rises that only ten years ago was rolling sand dunes by the sea. In my eight-year tenure here, I have witnessed the transformations and taken a joyride on Dubai's roller coaster. Today's Dubai remains the hip city: cool, futuristic, extravagant, experimental and continuously busy reinventing itself.

The design industry has grown to match the delirious speed of the urban developments. The young generation of Arab designers are pushing the boundaries and experimenting with one of the highly cherished cultural emblems - Arabic script. They are producing Arabic

نوافذ 12
الحسناء الإيطالية مونيكا
بيلوتشي زوجة دراكولا مجدداً

ملاعب 23
«السعادة» إلى أصحابها
والحزن يلازم «الملك»

نوافذ 48
ا السركال: محمد بن راشد
ألهمني ودعمني للمنصب

Wednesday
May 2007
emaratalyoum.ae

03

الإمارات اليوم

DUBAI

إيواء العمالة المخالفة خيانة وطنية

عرض استراتيجية الدولة: ووصف وزارات بأنها متخلفة وتفتقر للمنهجية

بتوجيهات صاحب السمو الشيخ محمد بن راشد آل مكتوم نائب رئيس الدولة رئيس مجلس الوزراء حاكم دبي، أطلق سمو الشيخ حمدان بن محمد بن راشد آل مكتوم رئيس المجلس التنفيذي بدبي أمس مشروع «يونيفرسال سيتي دبي لاند» الذي تنفذه «التطوير» العضو بدبي القابضة في إطار مشروع «دبي لاند» باستثمارات تصل إلى 8 مليارات درهم على مساحة 22 مليون قدم مربع ويتوقع انجازه عام 2010. ويعد المشروع الجديد الأول من نوعه في المنطقة مما يعزز مكانة المدينة على خارطة السياحة العالمية تجسيداً لخطة دبي الإستراتيجية 2015. وحضر حفل الإطلاق معالي محمد القرقاوي وزير الدولة لشؤون مجلس الوزراء، وسلطان بن سليم الرئيس التنفيذي لمؤسسة الموانئ والجمارك والمنطقة الحرة رئيس «نخيل» العقارية وعدد من الفعاليات الاقتصادية في الدولة. سليمع معبرا عن سعادته بإطلاق المشروع «سيتنافس «يونيفرسال» الأول من نوعه في المنطقة مما يعزز مكانة المدينة على خارطة السياحة العالمية تجسيداً لخطة دبي الإستراتيجية 2015. وحضر حفل الإطلاق معالي محمد القرقاوي وزير الدولة لشؤون مجلس الوزراء، وسلطان بن سليم الرئيس التنفيذي لمؤسسة الموانئ والجمارك والمنطقة الحرة ستي دبي لاند» 3 ملايين زائر سيأتون لزيارة أربع مناطق ترفيهية هي (هوليوود، ومتروبوليس، والمغامرات، والصور المتحركة). ويتكون المشروع من 5 .6 ملايين قدم مربعة وهثل. وقال سعيد المنتقل رئيس مجلس إدارة شركة تطوير عقب كلمة ألقاها في الحفل الذي شهد كلمة متلفزة للمخرج العالمي ستيفن سبليرع معربا عن سعادته بإطلاق المشروع. 08

جندي أميركي يعترف بإصداره أوامر مذبحة

بتوجيهات صاحب السمو الشيخ محمد بن راشد آل مكتوم نائب رئيس الدولة رئيس مجلس الوزراء حاكم دبي، ستي دبي لاند» الذي تنفذه «التطوير» العضو بدبي القابضة الدولة رئيس مجلس الوزراء، حاكم دبي، أطلق سمو الشيخ حمدان بن «يونيفرسال ستي دبي لاند» الذي تنفذه «دبي لاند» باستثمارات تصل إلى 8 مليارات درهم على مساحة 22 مليون قدم مربع ويتوقع انجازه عام 2010. ويعد. 24

تفجير شاحنة ملغومة يبدد استقرار أربيل

بتوجيهات صاحب السمو الشيخ محمد بن راشد آل مكتوم نائب رئيس الدولة رئيس مجلس الوزراء حاكم دبي، ستي دبي لاند» الذي تنفذه «التطوير» العضو بدبي القابضة الدولة رئيس مجلس الوزراء، حاكم دبي، أطلق سمو الشيخ حمدان بن محمد بن راشد آل مكتوم رئيس مجلس الوزراء حاكم دبي، الذي تنفذه «دبي لاند» مشروع في إطار «دبي لاند» باستثمارات تصل إلى 8 مليارات درهم على مساحة 22 مليون قدم مربع ويتوقع انجازه عام 2010. ويعد. 09

fonts that meet the needs of contemporary communications. In Dubai's visual culture the trend leans towards modern and streamlined typefaces on the one hand, and playful/conceptual experimentation on the other. I want to discuss the work of three designers that operate out of Dubai and for Dubai clients.

The first is Pascal Zoghbi, a type designer and founder of the recently launched independent Arabic font foundry *29LT*. He was one of the young generation of Arab designers that have brought the new trends in type design to the Arab Middle East. He has designed several custom fonts that have shaped Dubai's visual culture in inconspicuous ways. His first Dubai font was custom-developed for a campaign in the theatrical Ibn Battuta Mall. The Arabic font was designed to match an extra bold Futura (hence the name *Bukra*, meaning tomorrow in Arabic). This was the beginning of many more commissions that included the ubiquitous font for the newspaper *Emarat al-Yawm* (*Emirates Today*'s Arabic edition). The newspaper was rebranding its image to represent the younger generation of Gulf urbanites. The font was to represent a contemporary and dynamic image, while keeping the classical style of bold typefaces used in Arab newspapers, from his super bold to sturdy to the light font for the *Shawati* lifestyle magazine. This latter is a neo-Naskh style with Bodoni-esque qualities; its super sharp details and thick-to-thin contrast gives it an extravagant and quirky look worthy of our fashion-conscious Arabian city.

The cool, typographic city requires also an experimental dynamic type that represents its identity and the unexpected mixes of its vernacular languages. As a member of one of the teams working on the experimental type research project initiated by the Khatt Foundation (Typographic Matchmaking in the City, 2009-2011), Zoghbi's *Hamsa* (whisper) font, designed in collaboration with Erik van Blokland and Joumana Al Jabri, is a super thin mono-linear stencil font. This font's unusual design process began with creating 3D letters (made from sand water and wax) that mimicked construction techniques used in Dubai's urban developments. The design process led to the stripping down of all details, leaving only the structure of each form exposed. One could see again a reference to scaffolding and building foundations.

This same experimental typographic approach is evident in the work of Salem al-Qassimi, graphic designer and founder of Fikra design studio. In his conceptual projects he explores the potential of typography 'beyond print'. His font experiments can only live in 3D (cyber) space, they represent *Arabish* (a way of writing vernacular Arabic using English letters/numerals). His Arabic and Latin letters, like the cultures they represent, merge, detach and reattach to each other, in a randomly programmed animation, changing each time into different unexpected hybrid forms. The letters become 3D objects that invade the urban landscape and interact with the city's architecture, floating down from outer space like alien spaceships. This typographic experimental project is his personal representation of Dubai's cultural melting pot and its architectural hybridity.

Architecture and typography in Dubai are all about lines and geometry. They reinvent the rules and challenge conventionality. What seems like a simple idea (*fikra*) can be a blueprint for open-ended possibilities and complexity. The Fikra font is just that: it breaks with the stereotypical conventions of Arabic calligraphy, its pure geometry and the dynamic interplay between letters replace the fluid calligraphic strokes. Constructed from circles and lines, it provides the skeleton for many typographic possibilities and new designs.

It is a work in progress pushing the boundaries of acceptable illegibility. Al-Qassimi, takes this idea further in his Happy13 App, where a dynamically created sketchy/shaky font can be manipulated playing with the parametres of spread and speed, creating uncommon, random typographic animations. Both fonts emulate Dubai's state of flux and its uncontrollable organic growth.

The third and last independent designer is Lara Assouad Khoury, whose work marries beauty, function and conceptual experimentation. Her constructivist Tabati font is a mastery of control and ingenuity. Like a Zen master, she strips her typeface design to its barest essence, using the most basic geometric shapes, circles, squares and triangles, to build a complex typographic system that can be used for writing as well as drawing. She believes that "the Arabic script can be purist, minimalist and contemporary, and not always carry the burden of its historical calligraphic heritage". She created an Arabic font that relates to the urban world that surrounds us, thus demonstrating the limitless possibilities of Arabic typography. In their own way, all three designers reveal the multifaceted identity of Dubai—the delirious typographic city par excellence.

FAMOUS

TEXT: **REWA ZEINATI**

*"The bent photograph is famous to the one who carries it/
and not at all famous to the one who is pictured."*
Naomi Shihab Nye

Every day after work, instead of going home, where I lived alone
when I first arrived to Dubai, I would drive straight ahead on Sheikh
Zayed Road to meet some friends in a café that no longer exists
today; a popular and relatively less tattered hookah joint, with
large, outdoor seating space and dark, bamboo chairs with slightly
discoloured cushions.

I would look forward to not speaking, to listening, if Umm
Kulthum or Fayrouz were playing in the background. To simply
listening to others converse, argue politics, economics, raise their
voice momentarily, remember to look around, lower it back again,
laugh inwardly, sip their Moroccan tea. Their black tea with fresh
mint leaves. Their coffee. The smoke of our collective hookah
would blend in the air, the bubbling sound of the water in the glass,
strangely soothing. I would inhale deeply and exhale extendedly. I
would forget about the long drive to and from the office located in
Abu Dhabi.

Then: I did not grow up in Dubai. I grew up in Dubai's rich, older sister, at a time when Channel 33 was the only English Channel. My mother obsessed over *The Bold and the Beautiful*. We, the kids, watched *Beverly Hills 90210* and my parents would share this weekly hour with us, and discreetly offer their opinions regarding teenage problems revealed in each episode. We were teenagers at the time and the school was packed with expats. Perhaps this was our parent's way of watching over us.

Then: On the weekends we'd travel from Abu Dhabi, to that distant city of glamour, of business, of family-unfriendliness, where *a* mall existed. This was during the 90s; there was only one mall in Dubai. The trip took two hours from one Emirate to the next, and the scenery was less than remarkable. Endless stretches of flat, arid, beige terrains. Tiresome.

My mother would mention her longing for the mountains of Lebanon in all their glorious greenery. An image we all knew was only partially true.

I would spend the trip staring out the window, seeing nothing, listening to the sound of the speed alarm, ceaseless in its ring, announcing that my father was going over 120 km/hour. My father, unaffected, would continue the conversation he probably instigated.

Now: Too many malls for such a small city. Skyscrapers and glass towers and hotels and parks. The city expanded, stretched its highways, built its bridges and lengthy flyovers and never looked back. It was as if it was racing with its own idea of time and was adamant to win even against itself.

Now: But time has other ideas. It submits to nature. It stands still during the summer months. Dubai becomes a giant outdoor oven, continually open-mouthed. You spend hours indoors, indoors, indoors. You sleep to the drone of the AC on high. You escape to your car, to the office, to the gym, to your friend's place, to a bar, to the movies, to your couch. You escape to another country. In the summer, Dubai needs to be fled. The sky a suffocating shade of white. The air pierced by a bitter sun.

It becomes a city for sitting. A city that shuns pedestrians, mocks them, laughs at them, challenges their choices. A city that asks you to close the window, turn on the AC. Close the blinds, draw the curtains, turn up the music. Begin to forget the noise of unyielding construction work outside.

But when winter arrives, you find yourself forgiving the summer months. Forgetting almost. A winter that's an undecided mix of fall and spring. A combination of flip-flops and Christmas and long sleeves and tanning lotion, Spf 50. Winter is sitting by the creek, on the *other* side of all the glitz and exaggerated billboards, and watching the glittering boats pass by, some for tourists, some for items for trade. And enjoying the best *pani puri* in town.

On this side, Dubai's memory lives on. During the day, you inhale the scent of the cobalt blue sea. You collect shells off the shore. You build forts and drown them with seawater.

And you notice birds in winter; some a stunning shade of indigo, some a tinted red. Imported. Temporary. In the summer the birds don't fly high enough, weighed down by the dizzying heat, they risk crashing into windshields and car doors.

In December, you light a fire in the garden and pour a glass of South African wine, and roast chestnuts from China and pretend they're tasty. And sometimes they are.

Now: Dubai is a city for lovers. It doesn't mind if you love a man from another faith. Dubai doesn't mind if you love a man from a different background or homeland or morning ritual. Dubai doesn't mind. Is it the only Arab city that doesn't? Yes, it probably is. Dubai doesn't give you strange looks or side-glances or whispers behind your desperately indifferent back, or wonders about your family for

who you may have chosen. Dubai gives you the keys. With a tag that shows an expiration date.

It tells you, *I won't look, if you'll keep giving back.*

And you keep giving back.

Now: Dubai is a city for artists. A place that craves the written word, the spoken word, the line and curve, the secrecy and disarray. And it's packed with it. If you look closely enough, the city is packed with voices bursting to connect. Underground platforms where stories are woven and told and shared, and tears are shed in front of strangers where no one is deemed too vulnerable. As well as more mainstream, quieter settings, where words hide behind words. And everyone is at risk of exposure.

But exposure is what Dubai is all about.

Founders keepers.

Then & Now: They would be dressed in blue or yellow. Their faces covered with cloth, their heads under helmets. The sun beating down on their brown bodies. A law was made to keep the workers out of the scorching summer heat from 1 till 4 pm. And I don't remember a single face.

Now: Dubai is a safe city. Take a cab at 3am in high heels and a slinky skirt after a night out with friends in a club and you'll reach your door unharmed. Fear is a factor. So is trust. You trust that they are fearful.

I argue with the taxi driver in the middle of the day to slow down on the highway and he argues back. He has no time to waste, he knows what he's doing, if I don't like it I can step down and take another one. I inhale the AC-chilled smell of his cold, dried sweat. I look at the meter. This doesn't happen often.

I argue with the phone company that cuts my cable if I'm only a day late with settling my bills. They ask about their customer service and I have pages to share. I argue with myself about how convenient this city is. How it spoils you, draws you in, softens you. Makes you oblivious to everything else. Everyone else. If you let it.

Now: One day you're a foreigner, the next you're safe. You're in. You're one of the crowd. One day you're safe, the next you're an outsider. An intruder. Depending on the news.

And time. Time passes too quickly here. Too quickly. You plan on coming to Dubai for a year or two. You say you'll try it out, you'll see how it goes. But you're drawn to it, drawn in, drawn in, drawn in. Almost addicted. Maybe you left a marriage behind, maybe a war-torn country, maybe poverty, or dependence, or taxes. Or too much or too little of something. You say - *I'll try it out, what have I got to lose*? And just as easily nine or nineteen years go by.

What have I got to lose?

REVIEW

TO EACH THEIR OWN WORLDS

PHOTOGRAPHY: **JALAL ABUTHINA**

SRINU. SECURITY GUARD - CONSTRUCTION SITE, JLT. INDIAN

MOHAMMED. MUNICIPALITY WORKER - SUNSET (BURJ AL ARAB) BEACH. INDIAN

MOHAMMED. SALIK TOLL GATE SECURITY GUARD - SHEIKH ZAYED ROAD. BANGLADESHI

BELINDE. WATCHMAN - BUSINESS BAY. KENYAN

ANNELIE. CONSTRUCTION WORKER - PALM JUMEIRAH. SOUTH AFRICAN

KAMAL. DOORMAN AT A PAKISTANI RESTAURANT - BARSHA. PAKISTANI

JAMAL AND MOHAMMED. WINDOW CLEANERS - BARSHA. INDIAN

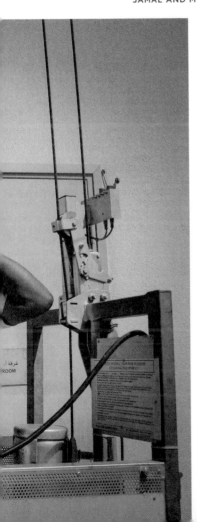

THE INVISIBLE
ENTREPÔT

TEXT: **JOHN ZADA**

IMAGES: **MOHAMAD BADR**

At first I barely registered his gaze: the subtle yet piercing look
of that almost nondescript, middle-aged man in the bluish-gray
shalwar kameez. I had no idea how long he'd been there. But from the
moment I noticed him he remained completely still, leaning against
a pile of rice bags, and staring in my direction with that unflinching
look of fascination so commonly directed towards visitors to the
East. He had the appearance a lone operator, who, in his strange
demeanour stood out in the sea of South Asian activity that unfolded
around us.

Just twenty feet away I was crouched down having tea with
an Indian from Gujarat. He was part of the crew of an old dhow
boat, docked near us, that had recently returned from a journey
to Yemen. Using a motley combination of broken Arabic (both of
us), kindergarten English (me), and a strange, ad-hoc sign language
(mostly him), we tarried in messy dialogue.

I was fishing for Sindhbadian tales from the man's seafaring
adventures. The Gujarati was explaining - as far as I could tell - that
someone on his boat had fallen overboard while at sea. But that was
all I could piece together. After that, his account became emotional

and I was unable to grasp the garbled, unintelligible details that followed. I shook my head and shrugged my shoulders indicating I had lost the thread. The Indian, in turn sighed, lit a beedi cigarette and stared into space. Our translation Olympiad had reached an impasse.

It was at that moment that the enigmatic man at the rice bags (who I'd momentarily forgotten about) made his move. He walked straight over and crouched down beside us. After issuing a polite "hello" he began speaking with the Gujarati in a shared tongue. There was a short back and forth between the two.

The newly arrived stranger then turned to me, and speaking in a tarnished English tinged with an accent, said calmly: "This gentleman would like you to know that his close friend fell into the sea during a voyage several months ago."

"I understood that much," I replied. "But there's more to the story, I think." "Yes," he continued. "Only one member of the crew witnessed this event. That witness, after calling the rest of the crew for help, told everyone that the fallen man, who had a great fear of mice, saw one, ran about, lost his balance and fell into the sea. Because the man could not swim they were unable to rescue him."

The Gujarati looked at me and bobbed his head in agreement. But his face was also marred by an increasingly dour look, showing a mixture of pain and rage. He had made that face earlier.

"Can you ask him why he looks angry now?" I asked the man.

"Our friend here thinks the witness is lying," he said, "he thinks the supposed witness actually struck his friend and threw him into the sea. The two argued often about money."

The strange tale raised more questions than it answered. Having no appetite to wade into murder allegations, I thanked the Gujarati for the glass of tea he had poured me and gave him my condolences. My enthusiastic translator stood up alongside me, and followed as I walked away.

"You are disturbed by this story," he said. "Things like this happen often. More than you know."

"Who are you?" I asked him, with a touch of annoyance that cloaked my growing curiosity.

"My name is Iqbal," he answered with slight aplomb. "I work here in the wharf. My father comes from Quetta in Pakistan. I would like to invite you for kebab at *al-Difaf* Restaurant across the street. Will you join me?

Having met my share of swindlers and touts across the region, and not entirely trusting him, I asked how he was able to communicate with the Gujarati if he was indeed Pakistani (an admittedly poor question if I was looking to catch him in a lie).

"Well, the languages of our two countries are similar. If you knew how similar, you wouldn't have asked this question. Humans too are not so different from each other. Don't be fooled by culture and politics."

This scene, which had become stranger by the moment, played out in one of Dubai's last holdouts of raw international culture. The city's Dhow Wharf, Dubai's secondary port and junior shipyard.

Dating back to the early 1800s, the wharf harbours an ancient type of sea-going ship known as the *dhow*. These traditional wooden sailing vessels, whose modern-day variants are rigged up with motors, are the primary vehicles used for small maritime trade in and around the Arabian Gulf.

The boats, laden with every imaginable commodity and commandeered by poor but intrepid crews of foreign sailors, make frequent journeys to and from neighbouring destinations of intrigue: Pakistan, Oman, Yemen, Iran, Iraq, Sudan and Somalia. The boat payloads range from spices and dried fruit to refrigerators and used auto parts. The life of a dhow worker is anything but easy. In addition to hard, round-the-clock grunt work loading and unloading boats, crews must run a gauntlet of tribulations while at sea, ranging from storms, to pirates to their own, sometimes surly, company.

The unruly cluster of aging wooden ships and their cargo, sitting on the edge of Baniyas Road - a veritable portal to and from other worlds - is to most residents an eyesore to be tuned out. The exigencies of modernity, materialism and the pursuit of glamour have rendered this old, worldly *entrepôt* all but invisible. I too fell into the same trap, nudged into indifference by the mouse-like ruts and five-star distractions of my new life that kept me from exploring this gateway of regional multiculturalism and grass roots commerce.

But one day I snapped out of my bubble-induced torpor. I was doing research for an article on the Iran nuclear issue when I came across an online report that alleged some technological hardware had been smuggled into Iran from across the Gulf - by way of a dhow boat from Dubai! I decided to go to the wharf the next day, for no other purpose than to see the little world that I had lazily neglected for too long. My encounters with the Gujarati and the inimitable Iqbal - and more - followed from that one decision.

A sort of casual friendship with Iqbal arose from that unusual meeting. I was suspicious of the man at first, but our shared feast of cheap biryani and grilled meats put my worries largely to rest. In our discussion, Iqbal demonstrated intelligence, worldliness, humour, insight and had a subtle flair for the humanitarian, which he would reveal in later meetings. But he also brimmed with ambiguities.

Iqbal described himself as a shipping 'agent' and partner to a wealthy dhow owner who had a small fleet of boats at the wharf. He claimed to sometimes travel with the ships to conduct "additional business" at certain destinations (he withheld details), or when the boat's payload was "extra-valuable".

I never saw him actually getting on, or off, a boat. Nor was I ever introduced to his partner or any of his regular colleagues. Iqbal

certainly knew people at the wharf and clearly had business dealings with them, taking or receiving money, packages or documents. He introduced anyone I ever saw him with at the wharf as "my friend" without further elaboration.

Clear details about his personal life were just as hard to come by. Iqbal never took me to his home, which he described once to me as "a small flat behind the souq" in Deira. He used the word "family" to refer to his seldom-mentioned relatives back in Pakistan. And he never once spoke of a wife. When I asked him later if he was married, he mumbled a few words about a relationship "long ago", then quickly changed the subject (though he did more than once speak, with an almost unguarded tenderness about a woman from Karachi now living in Dubai whom he was "helping"). Other questions related to his education and linguistic abilities also screamed out.

Suffice to say, certain things about him didn't add up. It wasn't altogether surprising or particularly important. Anyone in Dubai will tell you that the city hosts a legion of Houdini-types drawn from all over the world: escapees who've run away from war, poverty, boredom, spouses and sometimes themselves (was I one too?). As a result, some people look to forge completely new identities, or at least hope to conceal aspects of the old ones. Which is why many foreigners are guarded with the details of their past.

In the case of Iqbal, I quickly gained his trust by not being too nosey with him. Very soon he offered to be my unofficial guide to the older, South Asian populated neighbourhoods on the Deira side of the creek abutting the wharf. For people like myself who hadn't ventured much beyond the main avenues of that part of town, these were hidden corners of the city. I would go with him to these backstreets, pedestrian zones and souqs - natural extensions of the wharf - when I myself needed an escape.

One evening as we spoke at the wharf about the pleasures and pains of our inherited city, Iqbal, in a graceful stroke of spontaneity, broke our conversation with a slice of his hand in the air, saying, "Come with me. I want to show you something."

We made a journey through the car-crowded streets of Deira to a small 3-star hotel sheltered in a quiet cul-de-sac off one of the main thoroughfares. We walked through the bright, kitsch-studded lobby and into a long, brooding hallway throbbing with music. A large door at the end of the corridor led to a dark bar with a stage at the far end. About a dozen or so South Asian men sat at tables facing the stage. Above them were a group of musicians and a long line of Indian women dressed in colourful saris, sitting bored and restless on high stools. One by one the women would get up to do a kind of freestyle interpretive dance. Etched on the women's faces were expressions of forced enthusiasm and ennui. When an especially pretty or talented dancer hit the stage, any given man in the audience would purchase a bracelet (or two) to hand to the dancer. The woman would then smile, and put on the bracelet(s) and continue her dance while paying special attention to that man in the audience.

Another notable journey with Iqbal took place, months later, on my return from a weeklong assignment in Afghanistan. While away, I was exposed to the music of an iconic Pashto singer from neighbouring Pakistan named Haroon Bacha. The singer's melodies, primal and ethereal, became the soundtrack of an unforgettable road-trip in a pickup truck along the mountain road connecting Kabul and Jalalabad.

After leaving Afghanistan, I badly wanted the album. So when I returned to Dubai I went literally everywhere in my search to find it. No stone was left unturned in that obsessive hunt. And yet, strangely, no music store, regardless of how relevant its musical collection, carried it. Feeling dejected and that I had exhausted all my options, I ended the search.

A week later, while having tea again with Iqbal at the wharf, I had a sudden realization; one, which, I intuitively knew, would result in my getting my hands on that painfully elusive album: I would simply ask Iqbal. He was Pakistani. Surely, he'd know where I could find it.

Did he?

"Come," he replied without missing a beat.

For the next several hours Iqbal led me through a labyrinthine of stores hidden behind the tourist-trafficked souqs of Deira. Whole sections of that strange bazaar were devoted to single items: one street sold only doorknobs; another, pivoting wheels for office chairs and dollies; we later entered an alleyway that sold only knives. It was Dubai's little-known wholesaler district and it went on seemingly forever. Iqbal visited an assortment of random characters (some unsavoury, and all of whom he called "my friend"), exchanging money, messages, and backslapping laughs along the way.

As we walked along the street that sold salt-and-pepper shakers, a rare and sudden downpour caught us unawares. Iqbal grabbed my arm and led me immediately into a music shop that just happened to be at the corner ahead of us. When the storeowner greeted us and asked how he could help, Iqbal turned to look at me as if to say, "It's all yours."

I asked for the Haroon Bacha album. And low and behold, there it was (although I was given a cassette tape instead of a CD).

When we reached the wharf later, after a short detour through the Spice Souq, I expressed to Iqbal my disbelief at my inability to find the tape myself until I'd given up all hopes of finding it. My Pakistani friend stared at me and then shook his head and grinned.

"You think there is a mystery, when there is in fact none," he said cryptically. "In one sense, you just didn't know where to look. This had to be corrected. But there is also another aspect. And that something can be best conveyed in an expression.

"What's that?" I asked him, annoyed by his didactic tone.

He replied, "a famous man - a wise man from Delhi - long ago said - after seeking, you shall find. But you shall not find in the seeking." Iqbal then pulled out one of a bunch of dry dates in his pocket and popped it into his mouth. He looked at me as he chewed, smiling from ear-to-ear.

Friends in Dubai can vanish as quickly, and as easily, as they appear. And in a fashion that was hardly atypical for the city, Iqbal and I fell off each other's radars. In this case, I was mostly to blame. New friends, a spate of heavy travels and the demands of a new relationship diverted me for a period from the invisible entrepôt. The gravity of the city was moving increasingly westward following its developmental manifest destiny out into the deserts. It was those areas where I increasingly spent my time.

When I did finally reach out to Iqbal, some time later, his phone number was no longer working. A follow-up visit to the dhow wharf to look for him resulted in many look-a-likes, but no Iqbal. When I went to the café where we sometimes had tea, none of the new employees knew him. I managed to wrangle the manager, but he said he didn't know where Iqbal was. He hadn't seen him for months.

And so that was it. Like other casual friends and acquaintances in Dubai, Iqbal quietly made his exit, never to contact me again. He returned to the total obscurity from which he had so suddenly, and dramatically, appeared.

In the meantime, the dhow wharf, that charming holdout of an organic and historic maritime culture, has fallen to the cutting knife of the city's planners and plastic surgeons. In 2012, the Dubai municipality announced a multi-million dollar facelift-expansion of the wharf meant, in part, to increase trade and revenue for the city.

The unruly wharf, with all of its rugged characters, was finally going to be reined-in and co-opted into the machine of cleanliness and order that defines much of the 21st century UAE. The changes would no doubt confer benefits to the area as much as they would detract from its essence.

Yet, questions lingered. Will the dhow wharf be more - or less - invisible under its new, controlling tutelage? Will the living and breathing reality of its people and stories, concealed behind a new façade, still be discernible? Will it even exist as we used to know it? If not, then what, if anything, will be remembered of the area and its past? And what would Iqbal have to say on the matter?

Could his sudden disappearance be in some way connected to this inevitable change - as if he had intuited it and strongly disapproved? I still wonder.

A POET'S JOURNEY
THROUGH THE DIFC

TEXT: **FRANK DULLAGHAN**

PHOTOGRAPHY: **JALAL ABUTHINA**

The sun weighs on my shoulders and head as I stand with my back to the twin candles of Emirates Towers, looking across at the triumph of The Gate, that iconic building that is the mark of the Dubai International Financial Centre (DIFC). I come here to work, earn a salary. But on those days when I'm attuned enough to notice, I also come to be amazed. The architecture is clean and majestic, as suits a financial centre: the grand scale of it, the open spaces, the water, the lawns, the wide shallow steps – it's a place than can touch you if you're open to it.

The Gate draws my eyes up, as all imposing buildings are designed to do. I feel small in comparison, yet part of it. I can fit in here. I have a purpose. I have a job to go to. But I can also savour the moment of arrival, the imposition of place. I'm pleased to be here.

The Gate

is where the head goes when the heart stills -
the high gaze: this magnificence, this portal,
this gate to opportunity. It's also a way into
a place of work, of rules and regulation,
money making money making wealth.
Even the artist needs to earn a daily portion;
the heart must sometimes rest its questioning.

The heart must sometimes rest its questioning.
Even the artist needs to earn a daily portion -
money making money making wealth -
a place of work, of rules and regulation;
this gate to opportunity. It's also a way into
the high gaze. This magnificence, this portal
is where the head goes when the heart stills.

PARKING

As with most places in Dubai, parking can be a challenge. I tend
to get here early. But even early, the car park is almost full. I park my
battered Nissan in good company - two large 4 x 4s stand shoulder
to shoulder beside it like body guards, a sleek, silver, two-door Merc
shines next to the elevator doors, its owner no doubt already making
money. There are also three BMWs, a Chrysler 300 with darkened
windows, a large sterile looking white Lexus, and a cheeky little blue
Fiat that screeched past me, almost clipped my wing and ejected its
driver - a fumble of papers, briefcase and handbag - who flashed a
Sorry at me as she jogged for the elevator. I followed slowly after her,
yawning.

REFLECTIONS

The Gate is surrounded on three sides by the glass-faced Precinct.
This is where you will find the external foot traffic, the job-stressed,
the money-makers and job-seekers, the coffee shop workers and
cleaners, the new mothers bringing their private miracles back into
offices to prove that there is another life, though not everyone will
believe this. The Precinct is also where I find the glass façade holding
the bright reflection of the Emirates Towers, breaking them into
fractals, turning them into a different kind of art.

Sometimes after work, I like to stroll here, visit one of the
expensive galleries. There is no problem wandering in to have a look
around.

Good Evening Sir, is there something I can show you?

He has no idea what kind of car I have sleeping in the car park.

Through the gallery window –
a security man dozing.

I like the way the galleries mix the old and the new, established artists with those trying to make it happen. There's something uplifting about all of this art in a financial centre; something uplifting, until you start checking prices and realise that it's just economic sense: this is where the money is, the open purses. So a bit like that conundrum I find in myself – a mixture of the economic and the artistic, money and writing. But isn't that always the way it has been in the art world? It has always been a numbers game.

PEOPLE WATCHING

At other times I'll go to my favourite coffee house - Caribou Coffee. This may be for a business meeting with a client or colleague but mostly it's to watch people. Today, there's a bright, young man in a business suit commanding a meeting a few tables away. Three others sit listening to him as he talks. I can feel that edge to his energy, his enthusiasm, can tell he's sharp without hearing the words. I can read the body language, the faces around him. I'm pretty sure I used to be that young. I'm not sure I used to be that sharp.

relaxing coffee –
       beside every mug
       a mobile phone.

Now I watch a pretty, young woman pace up and down outside. She's dressed in a sharp business suit that is softened by a pale, pink blouse. She checks her watch. Frequently. She scans the approaching faces, left then right, then left again. But now she stops, has come to attention, she's alert, her eyes widening. She's no longer watching but seems to be waiting for something - some internal countdown, perhaps. And now she steps out, purposeful, confident, wonderful, and crosses the boulevard, her shoulder briefcase swinging. She

glances neither right nor left but walks at a steady pace, her head high.

Jill, a man's voice stops her. She slowly turns, smiles. He comes to her. He's tall, dark. *Fancy seeing you*, she says. And he stands in her shine, lit up, exalted, captured.

> in the rushing throng –
> a young couple fill
> each other's gaze.

THE BOULEVARD

Ah, *The Boulevard*. This is the pedestrian way that runs the length of the DIFC underground. It's where expensive watch and tailoring establishments rub shoulders with *Subways* and noodle houses. It has courier and car hire counters, printers and the *Registrar of Companies* office. This is a place worth the stroll, often for the small things that happen unexpectedly: a dark-eyed toddler smiling up at a white-clad Arab man; the small boy with the green balloon walking solemnly amongst all the suits.

> sitting high –
> the executive smiles
> as his shoes are shined.

IT'S NOT ALL ABOUT WORK

The strange thing about moving through the DIFC is often the snatches of conversation that juxtaposition themselves for your hearing.

I'm responsible for everything, I suppose ...

It's my best option at the moment ...

... trying to be helpful ...

We should close by the end of this week

How long before the money comes in?

Just unbelievable ...

I'm still waiting for him to call me.

and the background music drifting out of *Caribou*

... found love in a hopeless place ...

You could construct any kind of narrative around this. But, of course, you know where you are and so most of it is about money, about numbers, I suppose. But the numbers aren't always positive. I remember the days of loss when my company did not survive the global economic downturn, those unsettled days when the numbers were slipping, less sure of themselves, unable to find a way back to a best fit. It's not always possible to win. It's difficult sometimes even to survive. The world goes out of balance and you have to stop, wait for the tilt to right itself, before starting again, before stepping up from that new bottom to face the old failures and find fresh ways to go about your life. As the fund managers here will tell you, you need to spread your portfolio. If you invest too much of yourself in work you could be ruined.

I remember those days well. Sheik Zayed Road was suddenly lightened of its load of traffic, parking was almost a thing of joy, if you had a place to go to. So perhaps it's not so bad after all, to have to fight for a place in the car park, to wrestle with congestion. I make my way to my car at the end of another day and sit into its familiar capsule. I listen to it purr with pleasure for a short while before heading out onto the roads of Dubai.

DRAWN BLANK

TEXT: **FIONA PATTERSON**

PHOTOGRAPHY: **AB**

He's nearly a god.

BOO! IT'S THE NEW PLASTIC. Sprayed across a building site barrier facing our apartment block, at the entrance to Palm Jumeirah's long-overdue mall.

It was, of course, a sideswipe at credit card-wielding arrivistes (the people who showed up after us, of course).

And nothing short of miraculous, just a day after I'd commissioned Arcadia Blank to produce some comment on our stretch of the Trunk.

'Ma'Shaa'Allah', as it says on the bumper stickers here.

I'd first encountered Blank's work when I moved to Dubai with my husband in 2011.

Both of us had misgivings about leaving the UK. A distant relative who'd lived in the UAE fifteen years ago said he'd struggled to fill his diary. "There's no critical mass, no culture."

Before finding an apartment, we stayed at a place in TECOM (Technology, Electronic Commerce and Media), one of the affordable counterweights to the 'old' Dubai in this dumb-bell shaped city. It has an unusual road layout, like a flower - throwing curves at boy racers – but little else appealed to my desiccated eyes.

The view from our room was bleak: no finished buildings or landscaping, just a vast, swirling junction with vehicles fleeing in all directions. Venturing into the Marina and Jumeirah Lakes Towers at the 'new', southern end of Dubai, I was shocked at the raggedy edges, the way that none of the developments interlocked. It looked so random, like a toy building set thrown to the floor. Not knowing the void that preceded it, nor the disruptive plans for a new metro system, Dubai seemed rickety, barebones. It was a big contrast to the hedgerows, history and close-set London streets I'd left behind.

I missed the street art, too: awesome works from the likes of David Mach, Antony Gormley and, with my brother living in Bristol, Banksy. We always pointed out his stencilled window with its raging couple, the husband overlooking his wife's lover dangling from the sill.

But Banksy aside, I found most other UK graffiti banal: brain-dead scribble on every municipal surface. Why not throw us some one-liners? Make us think; make us laugh.

Laughs were rare as I got to grips with Dubai. I'd arrived grieving after my mother's death, with an ankle injury. All the usual props were kicked away - family, friends, home, Private Eye, Radio 4.

And then I saw: PLASTIC DREAMS AND PRIMAL SCREAMS on a TECOM hoarding.

I asked the cab driver to slow down so I could snap it on the way to Arabic classes in Knowledge Village (you know where you are in the new Dubai: Business Bay; Motor City; Silicon Oasis).

Plastic Dreams: yes, the hope instilled by selective camera angles (Dubai looked so shiny in the brochures), and Primal Screams? The hollowing swoosh: reality.

The 'A' in Screams sat below the line. It looked like a triangle and a tag, also the Arabic 'Taa Marbuta' or 'tied T', denoting femininity. Was the artist female? Those were my first impressions. And art means whatever you make of it, after all.

Blank's subversive little messages gave me huge hope: this place has a pulse, maybe even a conscience. Wit, dissent, originality: things worth sticking around for. All of which sustained me through my first few confronting months amid the dusty back lots and corporate canyons.

In my weakened state, I was highly susceptible to the other drawn 'Blanks' I found. Like a punter in a fortune-teller's tent, I was being fed lines that rang exponentially true. I began to think some maverick deity had me under surveillance.

Within a few weeks of arriving I cracked a tooth on a peppercorn. The dentist who looked at my teeth said they'd all shatter if I didn't straighten them out. Next to the dental surgery on Al Wasl Road (a long, Californian tract of cosmeticians and marbled villas), Blank wrote: SMILE, YOU'RE DISINTEGRATING.

When I had braces fitted, I'M SO PLAIN appeared on barriers along Al Sufouh Road, flanking its array of mega-palaces. WE'RE NEARLY GODS, again in TECOM, as I flicked through the 'Ahlan

100' (Dubai's 'Who's Who'), and began to feel like an extra on an occasionally glamorous film set.

YOU'RE NUMB AGAIN when I went to the Roads and Transport Authority to get a replacement licence, and was told to walk the length of a vast, echoing corridor to bring back a ticket for queuing. Alone.

On a rare excursion to Deira for an Arabic class: THE RAPTURE AIN'T COMING, and just over the road from that: LIGHT CAN'T ALWAYS BREAK THROUGH. Anyone who's tried to learn the language will understand. Was I the only one seeing these words, the only one ascribing any meaning to them?

I began writing down and photographing every line, thinking I'd piece together some sort of scripture.

Then new sightings began to dwindle. Which probably had as much to do with my closed circuit existence as anything else. Us southerners don't venture creek wards much: Dubai's a 'two halves' city, like London (I now know someone on Emaar Boulevard, which runs around the Burj Khalifa. She may as well be in Tehran).

Among the last signs I saw was: METATRON IS BORED on a barrier near Dubai Garden Centre. Ironically I'd just found several compelling places in Al Quoz with a visiting friend: The Courtyard, with its Ottoman Palace, 'Petals' (all up for sale), the Jamjar (which encourages you to sit and paint) and Al Serkal Avenue, a warehouse complex of stylish galleries.

NO SCENE loomed at me from a huge hoarding in Barsha as I struggled to meet like-minded people. And then nearby I stumbled into Ductac at the Mall of the Emirates, full of actors, writers and comedians.

The panoramic EVOLVE, each of its letters sprayed on the exposed ends of massive concrete columns disappeared when they were upended to support a new Metro line.

Then: ONE LAST GLIMPSE, on the side of a makeshift shed by a Palm service road, was dismantled. Blank's influence on me ebbed as I began to connect with my surroundings.

But by his very absence he still seemed pretty godlike. An arty friend, with her own scene and satellites, handed me the phone at the junction behind the LuLu hypermarket in Barsha, the one that always clogged up as we headed for our Saturday belly dance class.

"Here he is. Talk to him. He doesn't realise the effect his stuff has on people."

I hesitated at the offer of a hotline to the almighty. My face might melt off.

But I couldn't resist. Without any greetings, essential in the Arabic world, words just tumbled out.

As ever when I try to talk to celebrity, I lost it.

In a restaurant once, all I could think to say to John Hurt (*1984, Midnight Express*), sitting nearby, was that drunks always have great hair. "It was in the papers today! Their livers can't process the hormones in meat." Then I realised Mr. Hurt had impressive tresses. Thankfully my boyfriend intervened.

Given my big chance with Blank I had the blinding idea of recommending ways he could monetise his art:

"How about T-shirts? Scarves? There aren't enough good souvenirs here. You've seen 'Exit Through the Gift Shop'?"

Possibly the worst things you could say to a groundbreaking activist. Looking back, I'm surprised he didn't cut me dead.

Then I asked him to create a piece of graffiti just for me, on the Palm. I suggested "WHAT A VACANT LOT".

"No, that's your line."

He said he'd think about it. I handed the phone back as the traffic freed up. Realising my insanity I felt crushing regret.

That turned into euphoria when the bespoke Palm message

appeared at dawn. That evening I sent my dancing friend a photo: proof. "He puts the hours in. Thank him for me, won't you?"

Later my friend told me that the barrier hadn't been sprayed on the Palm. It had arrived from its original location via several other parts of the city. And by 'boo' to the new plastic, Blank meant he preferred the old red and white concrete barriers to the new hollow ones. Concrete clings on to spray paint: plastic just shrugs it off in the heat.

But I wasn't too vexed at this dashing of hopes and hypotheses. Having moved around repeatedly, 'my' barrier has become a nomad, the fleeting essence of Dubai: even more of a treasure.

Rather than hauling it into our apartment I'm leaving it for you to enjoy. Catch it soon, before the message peels away forever.

LIMINAL

PHOTOGRAPHY: **RICHARD ALLENBY-PRATT**

ABANDONED PROPERTY DEVELOPMENT

DESERT VILLAGE

FUNCTION VENUE

CAR LOGISTICS, JEBEL ALI FREEZONE

TOMORROW, I LEAVE

TEXT: **AMINA ABDEL-HALIM**

It's the morning call to prayer that wakes me up, it rattles me in what feels like the deep recesses of the night. Outside my window I see the silhouettes of a few steadfast souls scurrying about in the darkness towards the mosque next door, discarding their shoes in two swift motions and dissolving beyond the border of its arched entrance. I roll over and stare at the ceiling.

I've worked in many cities, and in Dubai work doesn't truly kick into gear until around 11am. People will book conference rooms and order full intricate breakfasts of eggs, *lebneh* and falafel. They'll have their Nescafé, smoke their cigarettes, and as much as they rush on the highway to get there, the journey to actually getting something done is slow paced. I only have a small pocket of time before the city comes to life under the blaze of the scorching sun, so I yank myself out of bed.

The air is still warm and humid when I step out, but much more bearable than it will be later in the day. If I head left I can walk all the way to Sheikh Zayed Road, but I'm headed right, towards water, with one stop along the way. Walking is something you can miss in Dubai. Not the kind of walking done frequently in malls or in the lobbies of

fancy hotels, but the kind of earthy walking you do under wide-open skies.. It's strange to admit now, but I remember feeling nervous the first couple times I did this. What if someone sees me wandering aimlessly by the road at this time?

It didn't take long to get over this momentary lapse in unnecessary self-consciousness and make peace with the fact that I'm on a one-woman mission involving carbs and sand.

My path doesn't have a name. It's a thin vein of sandy road that skirts Safa Park and spills out onto Al Wasl Road where the lights of Al Reef Lebanese Bakery beckon. Al Reef runs 24-hours on the buzz of Arabic Keebler Elves kneading, flouring and firing *mana'eesh*, flat breads similar to pizza without the red sauce. When I step inside I'm greeted with the warm familiar scent of yeast dough baking in a brick oven. The bakers' uniforms remain consistent: white shirts, white pants and white paper hats—white like the dough they work with all day. Like members of a secret club there are only a few fully functioning residents in the city at this moment and we happen to be among them.

I've heard tales of some more courageous souls ordering a concoction called 'Spicy-Meaty-Cheesy', but I always get a *Zaatar* and cheese *man'oushe*, a mix of dried thyme, olive oil and *akawi* melted together in perfect unison. It's folded in half and handed to me in a veil of wax paper, with a confident nod from the guy behind the counter. It's warm and soft as I head to the back fridge and search for an orange juice box labelled 'Milco'. Made of sugar, water and flavouring there are no health benefits to this orange drink, but I went to school in Abu Dhabi and we drank it in the cafeteria at lunch with chicken salad sandwiches and Ali Baba chips, so I drink it for old times sake.

It is brighter when I make my way outside and walk towards the gulf to find a spot on the shore. Sand can hold the sun's heat captive for an entire day, but at this moment it's cool to the touch and easy to nestle into. You can sit comfortably and watch fisherman in the distance, sometimes catching a glimpse of a net cast out with a whoosh against the sky, falling gently onto the liquid below. I like it now. It's still and quiet and I can take deep breaths.

The Dubai Sailing Club is far off to my right and on some days I'll spot a miniature fleet of pastel painted instructor boats bobbing out on the horizon. The water here is the kind of blue you see in travel magazines. The ones that feature tropical destinations like the Bahamas and the Caribbean. In the summer the water is too warm to swim in, at least for me, but in the coolness of winter you can sometimes spot little fish swimming below you as you make your way past the shore into the cool liquid blue.

Later in the day the beach will be studded with a mix of sunburnt tourists and expats, families sitting on large mats, a few women dressed in black from head to toe, some in shalwar kameez or just shalwar, traditional garb worn by a few Indo-Pakistani expats, but I only stay long enough to worry that I may be late for work.

Iqbal is a taxi driver that takes me to the office. Unlike other cities, it is very likely to hop in a cab in Dubai only to find that the driver is new. Iqbal however is able to navigate his way through side streets and back alleys only to pop out, just minutes from my office building on Sheikh Zayed Road.

On our first ride together I randomly hopped into his taxi and after reaching our destination in less than 15 minutes I asked if he wouldn't mind picking me up everyday. He nodded with a "sure sure" and it was a done deal.

In broken English Iqbal tells me stories of his family in Pakistan. He's supporting his wife and mother, that means most of the tip and wages he earns is sent to them. He tells me he's looking forward to going home to see them and that he only gets to do this twice a year.

"You must miss them," I say, and he nods politely. "My family's in America. I miss them too."

If there's an accident on the road, we talk about it, or more likely, I hear Iqbal mumble disapprovingly about it. "People, too fast driving," he says, as he shakes his head in the same way my father would if I walked out of the house with a shirt too tight or a skirt too short. When I get a cold and can't go to work I make sure to call Iqbal. He's set his call waiting to a prayer in Arabic, asking God for mercy and protection. If there's a sand storm or if it's unseasonably cool we'll talk about the weather, but sometimes Iqbal and I sit in silence as he vigilantly keeps track of the traffic and I stare out the window.

Sheikh Zayed road is a long stretch of highway bound by a multitude of roundabouts. In its simplest form, I think of it as a large semi-opened scroll, straight in the middle and curled at the ends. It's easy to navigate, but a person can get lost in the round bits, spinning off into one incorrect exit after another, which has happened to me many times.

High rises and buildings, both famous and unknown, flank its either side. Sometimes the sun ricochets against the glass panelling forming rainbow prisms that remind me of *that* Pink Floyd album. At other times the buildings tuck themselves into heavy blankets of cloud cover, disappearing into a mysteriously thick haze heralded in by the latest sand storm.

On the days Iqbal can't make it, he sends a cousin or a friend. When I give a larger than average tip he says: "No madame, too much." He is dependable and consistent - the perfect part of a morning spent searching for grounding in a city that changes on you as fast as the sand shifts.

I remember my friend referring to it as a heartbreak city. That so many people come in, and just when you get used to having them around, they go out. In the end it is me who sweeps in and out of this city.

I only attempt to tell Iqbal on my last day of work, on our last ride together.

"Tomorrow, I leave Iqbal. Taxi no need."

"No need madame?" he says.

"Yes, no need. I leave."

"Ah...okay, okay...good luck madame."

I smile awkwardly and wave like a child who's just been taught how to say goodbye, "You too Iqbal. Thank you."

AL REEF LEBANESE BAKERY
ADDRESS: JUMEIRAH, SAFA PARK.
OPPOSITE POST OFFICE
TEL: 04 396 1980

DUBAI OFFSHORE SAILING CLUB
ADDRESS: JUMEIRA 3
TEL: 04 394 1669

RECREATE

PHOTOGRAPHY: **BASILE MOOKHERJEE**

CARPET SHOPPING FROM A TO Z

TEXT: DENISE HOLLOWAY

A while back I heard a thing on the radio about Chess Boxing. The sport consists of men alternately punching each other in the head and trying to outwit the other at chess. I guess the point of this sport is to award both brawn and brains.

Shopping for a carpet is much like Chess Boxing, only more brutal. I've never been involved in a violent act while buying a carpet, although there have been times when either I or the carpet merchant, or both, were entertaining fantasies involving the other that would make Dario Argento blush.

Carpet buying is a blood sport in the sense that how much you pay depends as much on what you're made of, as it does on the value of the piece you're buying. Be spineless, overly friendly and willing to please and you are likely to overpay so much that your name may be inscribed alongside those who have bought the Brooklyn Bridge in that great ledger of foolish commercial transactions in the sky. Understand how the game is played and you will acquire a piece that will be a joy to you forever at a price that is fair to both you and the dealer.

The key to carpet shopping is the answer to this question: why are none of the pieces ever priced? The answer is simple. Unlike other

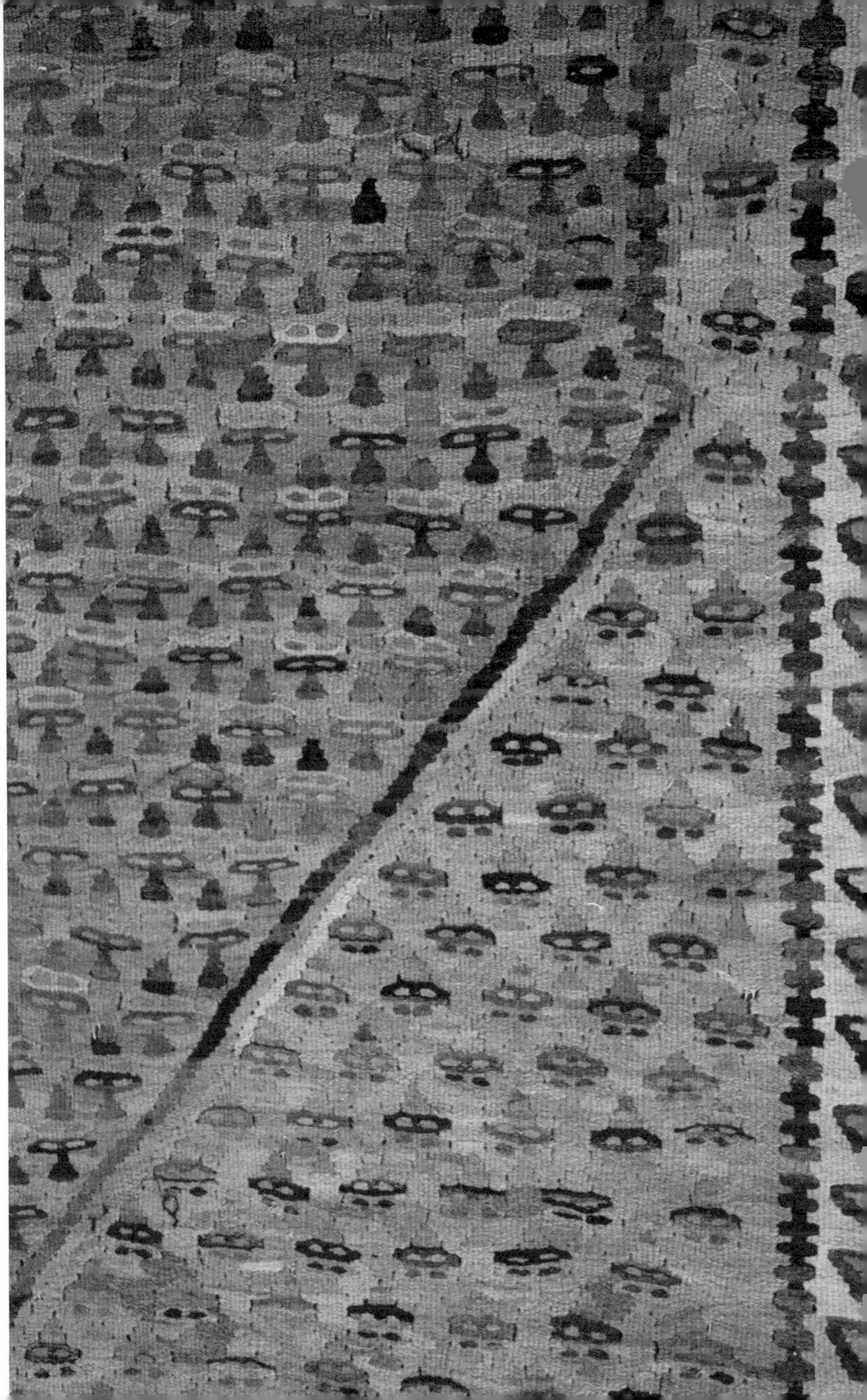

A SENNEH FROM IRAN

goods whose price is a function of the sum of the cost of inputs plus a profit margin, the price of a carpet is a function of quality, age, uniqueness and scarcity, but also of how much you, the potential buyer, think it is worth. As such, there is nothing morally suspect in the world of carpets if someone pays much more than the lowest price the dealer was willing to sell the piece for. This subjective method of determining a fair price, this piece of archaic capitalism that forms the basis of pricing carpets, was at first frustrating and then became beautiful to me.

When I first arrived in Dubai, my favourite carpet shopping was down in the Blue or Central souk in Sharjah (which is a city contiguous with Dubai, so only the most pedantic will quibble with its inclusion here). This souk fit the romantic (and yes, now embarrassingly Orientalist) notions I entertained about the Middle East before living here. The place was full of wood artefacts, silver work, stone carvings and carpets from Iran, Afghanistan, Pakistan, Central Asia, and India. Sure, a lot of it was touristy kitsch, but there was more than enough authenticity to make me feel I was exploring the newest stop on the Silk Road.

In a city of transients making friends is easy and I soon found two women, A and Z, whose love of carpets and textiles matched my own. Friday is the first day of the weekend in the UAE and so after Friday prayers, with or without our respective families, A, Z and I would have a lunch of *Musakhan, Lahori Beef Karahi* or *Ash-e Anar*[1] and then go carpet shopping.

Carpet shopping is an ancient art form that follows a set ritual of long and noble tradition. You are seated. Tea is served. Carpets are taken from stacks and spread open before you. The process is slow

---

1. MUSAKHAN IS A PALESTINIAN CHICKEN DISH, LAHORI BEEF KARAHI IS A PAKISTANI DISH, AND ASH-E ANAR IS IRANIAN POMEGRANATE SOUP.

and languid. Many dealers in Dubai come from a long line of carpet merchants, some going back generations. And because they want to match what they will charge you with what you are willing to pay, carpet dealers tend to know as much about human psychology as they do about carpets. A good dealer will know what you're looking for and how much you know about carpets by those you wave away. Finally, with a small pile of selected carpets in front of you, the real shopping begins.

During those long sessions I learned how to look at a carpet. I learned to identify country of origin, materials (silk, wool, wool on cotton, silk in cotton etc.) the density of the knots, intricacy of design and dye composition. With more practice these elements broke down into even finer detail: was the piece city, village or tribal? Was it new, vintage or antique? Did it use natural, plant based dyes, chemical dyes or both? Was it in perfect condition or had it been repaired? If the dealer was presenting the piece as an old carpet was it really an old carpet or had it been chemically washed, tea rinsed, left on the road and run over by large trucks or faded in the sun to make it look old? Was the abrash (variation in dye lots usually found in tribal rugs with plant based dyes) real or had it been manufactured?

What took longer to learn was how not to act like an excited teenager at a Justin Beiber concert each time I saw a piece I liked. A and Z had two diametrically opposite methods of negotiating price. Z used the velvet glove over a fist of steel approach. She exudes charm from every pore. Her voice is always sweet and polite. I've never seen her frustrated or raise an eyebrow. Slowly over hours or even days, the dealer realises that she will not be swayed from the price she is prepared to pay for a piece. What is worst, he realises that she is in for as long a game as it will take. We've gone back to the same shop multiple times when she found a carpet she liked. And the dealer, realising that he cannot be rude to so charming a woman, understands that his life for the foreseeable future, and perhaps forever, will consist of drinking tea with Z and talking about why the price she is willing to pay is the right price for this carpet and how there can be no other price. Unless, of course, he just accepts her offer. They almost always invariably do.

A uses the sphinx method. She asks questions. Inquires about this and that, and then initiates a long period of silence. During these periods she is transfixed on the carpet or examines the dealer or fusses with her phone, until the situation is so awkward, the dealer speaks. The dealer suggests a price, A rejects it and the cycle begins again and again until the right price is agreed.

When I first started buying carpets, dealers would give me gifts with my purchase. I took these gifts to symbolize how important a customer I had become to the dealer. Either that or the dealer was so impressed by my knowledge that he felt impelled to give me a tribute. Z and A never received a single gift from any dealer. I later realised that these gifts were pity prizes. The dealers had made so much profit from me that they showered me with whatever bobble was within reach in an attempt to assuage their guilt. I was devastated. I was no less devastated when I discovered that all stories the dealers told me about the lives of the weavers, that it took five weavers five years to make a carpet, or that the design in a carpet represented the hopes and dreams of the weavers, were bald faced lies. Most carpets on sale, anywhere in the world, are woven from graph paper patterns (cartoons) sold to the individual weavers or manufacturing houses. No one fetishises women's work quite like a carpet merchant and no one wanted to buy the stories more than I did.

Carpet merchants are descendants of a merchant class selling the same product for hundreds of years. The way they carry on their business, like each carpet they sell, is a present manifestation of a world whose origins can be traced through magnificent trade routes

LEFT: POGO WALKS ACROSS A SOUMAK RUG FROM DAGESTAN.
BELOW: A WELL-WORN AFGHAN PRAYER CARPET.

that continue to function after millennia. I was fortunate to fall under the guidance of one older Afghan gentleman that, beyond a few words, I did not share a common language with; sadly his shop is now dark and shuttered. Over the years I would show up at his shop, friends and family in tow and sit as he opened rug after rug. His first price was always within reason and he was a joy to bargain with. He would indicate the country of origin and repeat the name of the tribe or region over and over, until I could finally recognize them on my own. He would point out the markers that differentiate a Baluch from a Turkoman, a Qashqai from a Bakhtiyari, and often open up a map of Iran and Central Asia in case I was unsure. I was, on occasion, invited to share lunch with him and his family in a tiny apartment filled with so many stacks of rugs that there was barely enough floor space to spread out the food.

One day, I took Imad, an Afghan Canadian friend on a short stop over en route to Kabul where he was shooting a film, to see my favourite shop. With the language barrier gone the merchant rapidly recounted his story - first wife and six children had been killed in a bombing. He had only one surviving daughter from that marriage, she was married, still in Afghanistan and life was extremely difficult. He insisted that we come home with him for lunch but we were on a tight schedule. That day there was tea but no carpets, I think he felt a need to be finally, truthfully understood.

After ten years of hunting and buying, I have gained a modest collection scattered around our home. Like any collector - nascent or experienced - the carpets have become more than just domestic things; each piece represents a mark along a wonderful journey in wool and madder and indigo. The hard, tiled surfaces of our house have been softened and the echoing sounds of the concrete rooms, muffled. Truly understanding the world of carpets is a life long pursuit. This region has opened up in unexpected and unusual ways.

I see shapes, colours, countries, tribes and arbitrary borders when I think about the weaving regions I love. Regardless of faith, there is nothing as calming as placing your hands, knees and forehead into the well-worn imprints of an old prayer carpet. The bottomless cups of tea have led me into the homes and lives of some of the amazing people who sell me carpets, which if now are not close friends, then at least very special acquaintances. I have wandered the souks of Iran, Turkey, Syria and North Africa looking for the pieces closer to their source. If this has read like a cautionary tale, don't let it be. Open your eyes, find what you want and take hold of the narrative.

MY RECOMMENDATIONS:

MIRI CREATION

THE FIRST NEW PIECE I BOUGHT WAS A MIRI CARPET, FROM THEIR AUTHORIZED DEALER IN A LITTLE SHOP IN THE DUBAI CROWN PLAZA CONCOURSE. MIRI NOW HAS A LARGE SHOP IN THE LOWER LEVEL OF THE DUBAI MALL AND PLEASE DO NOT LET THEIR MALL LOCATION TURN YOU AWAY FROM WHAT, I BELIEVE, ARE THE FINEST CARPETS COMING OUT OF IRAN. THE MIRI FAMILY TAKE THEIR COMMITMENT TO THE CONSUMER AND TO THEIR CRAFT VERY SERIOUSLY – HAND SPUN WOOL, ALL NATURAL DYE, METICULOUS ATTENTION TO DETAIL AND QUALITY. IF YOU LOVE PERSIAN CARPETS, AS I DO, BUYING A MIRI CREATION WILL NOT ONLY INSURE THAT YOU ARE GETTING THE BEST QUALITY FOR PRICE ON THE MARKET BUT WILL ALSO SUPPORT A COMMERCIAL ENTERPRISE THAT HAS AN OBSESSIVE MISSION TO THE CONTINUATION OF THE ART OF THE PERSIAN CARPET AT ITS HIGHEST FORM.

SHOP # 97-2, LOWER GROUND FLOOR, THE DUBAI MALL, FINANCIAL CENTRE ROAD, DOWNTOWN BURJ KHALIFA.

LANDMARK: OPPOSITE MORELLI'S GELATO, ZIP CODE: 7597, CITY OF DUBAI.

TEL: 04 434 0433

AL MADAEN

THIS IS A SHOP WITH A FANTASTIC RANGE OF ANTIQUE, VINTAGE AND NEW CARPETS. MOST OF THEIR RUGS COME FROM IRAN BUT THEY ALSO HAVE A VERY GOOD SELECTION OF AFGHAN AND PAKISTAN PIECES. THE OWNERS, A FATHER AND SON TEAM, HAVE AN EXHAUSTIVE KNOWLEDGE OF THE PIECES THEY SELL AND HAVE THE BEST TRIBAL CARPET COLLECTION IN THE CITY.

AL HUDAIBA STREET, SATWA.

TEL: 04 345 4488

STYLE TRIBES

TEXT: **DIYA AJIT**

PHOTOGRAPHY: **LAFI**

What always strikes me first about a place is its smell - a palpable sensation of a place and its people that you can feel and taste even before you see it. Sweat and muddied smog in Mumbai or chocolate confections and freshly cut grass in Geneva. Dubai doesn't really have a scent. It's an amorphous canvas that is tinted with life and colour by its inbound inhabitants. A city forever in transition that has yielded an eclectic sartorial landscape.

At first glance it would appear that one can only find designer garb or cookie-cutter high street wares in Dubai. The trouble is that the most visible shopping options are concentrated in the malls. This forces the sartorially inclined to get creative, to look deeper and, eventually, to adopt an eclectic high-low approach to dressing by

mixing the somewhat mandatory luxury label purchases with high-street items. The result is a city of equally distinctive style tribes.

There's the Emirati women, swathed in black chiffon, donning Tom's canvas flats and clutching bejewelled designer handbags and sunglasses. There are the hot messes in H&M rayon miniskirts and vertiginous platforms. There's the creative types who, if asked, will tell you they buy their striking clothes on eBay or in children's shops 'back home'. The region's nascent fashion industry has also yielded a burgeoning group of local couture designers, bloggers, fashion victims, trendsetters and posers who can be found smouldering or pulling fish faces at the city's glamorous fashion events and private parties.

Just like this city where I was born, I am a chameleon - an ever-adapting character who is a little bit like everybody here which adds up to me being nothing like anyone else at all. Dubai was nothing but a cosy sandpit when I was a Benetton-wearing tyke growing up here. My mother worked in the travel industry and would shop for clothes for me on summer vacations in London. So limited were the shopping options that one of my earliest memories includes lusting after a hideous pair of marbled pink flats at the only decent shoe store in Dubai in the late 80's: Shoe Mart. I would be beside myself with anticipation for a trip to the Sana shop in downtown Karama whose catchy radio jingle 'Dress me up Saaannnaaa' would play on endless rotation on the drive to school, sandwiched between the latest tracks from *Wham!* and *New Kids on the Block*. I caught the fashion bug early, my mother still jokes that I'd wear her high heels and pearls to go to the toilet and of how I was so bewitched by the silk-satin of my ballet slippers that I'd sleep with them under my pillow. My father once bought me a pair of Bally men's shoes on a trip to the US and I wore them with everything from floaty summer dresses to baggy jeans. The BurJuman shopping mall opened when I was a teenager and I took to skulking around Mango, Zara and Diesel and begging my mother to buy me skinny jeans, tailored blazers and cherry red boots. Dubai's transformation from small, sleepy town to city came hard and fast. By the time I'd returned to the city after pursuing a degree in film abroad, it was a heaving consumer hub with every imaginable brand name screaming out to you from billboards, store fronts and gleaming facades of freshly erected skyscrapers. My little hometown was now home to 2.1 million people.

Many large malls had sprung up, each hosting mile upon mile of designer stores, forgettable repetitive high street goods and nauseatingly bright lights. I developed a deep aversion to the malls, instead I tried to find some trace of uniqueness, something real. I traipsed the old souqs for hours for exotic fabrics to make my own clothes, embraced online shopping, scoured the clutch of local vintage stores and flea markets and hunted for hours on Facebook groups. And then, in February of 2004, S*uce boutique opened.

Walking into S*uce in 2013 with its interiors plied with pink diamanté bows and selection of blindingly bright garments and accessories one could be forgiven for thinking that this is probably 'typical' of Dubai's boutique store offerings. I like to think of S*uce's selection as an almost satirical take on Dubai's ethos - S*uce serves up a heady dose of regional designer labels and statement contemporary labels from around the globe, all aligned in their seeming intent to exaggerate or make humour of excess with blatant graphic prints of gargantuan jewels or Riviera holidays, bold colours and plentiful use of leather, silk, beads and crystals. S*uce is also home to up-and-coming local labels such as Mochi who style traditional Rajasthani embroideries into covetable blazers, skirts and crop tops. It's costly being ironic though and S*uce, while being one of Dubai's oldest and best-loved boutiques, can still cause me heartbreak when I'm faced with the option of eating tinned beans all month for a ironic Tee.

Much of my time in the UAE has been spent looking for things on the fringe, things that are outside of this crazy bubble. I love off-roading and camping in the neighbouring Emirates of Fujairah and Ras Al Khaimah and sharing a shisha and café table with elderly men in rural Oman who tell stories of the old days and the 'old ways'. While there's no dearth of fashion designers in Dubai, Madiyah Al Sharqi, daughter of the Ruler of Fujairah, U.A.E, HH Sheikh Hamad bin Mohammed Al Sharqi, is also on my radar. You'll find her latest collections at Symphony Boutique in Dubai Mall alongside other regional designer talent such as Razan Alazzouni, Reem Juan, Malaak and Maryam Omaira. Here, a carefully edited selection of luxury international labels, shoes and accessories is housed in a large, glossy store with boudoir-style private changing rooms. It's refreshing to rub shoulders with veiled Emirati women as you browse through the rails of couture and contemporary wares and Symphony, along with Level Shoe District, manages to be one of the few places in Dubai Mall that makes it worth the blisters garnered by trekking through kilometres of retail space.

Working in the media industry from film to advertising, to public art and more recently a foray into the fashion industry has made me fortunate enough to meet some of the zaniest, creative people living in the Gulf. Enter Alia Korayem - a Saudi native who has spent much of her life in Los Angeles. Seeing a gap in the market for affordable, one-of-a-kind urban fashion and small contemporary labels, she launched the West L.A. boutique in 2012. This 2-room store in Sunset Mall on Umm Suqeim Road is packed to the rafters with clothes, shoes and accessories for the woman looking to stand out from the crowd. West L.A. is the place to go for statement sunglasses and distressed denim but also for striking party wear and beachwear.

There's plenty of fashion treasure to be found in Dubai. Hoards of vintage finds can be had at Garderobe on Jumeirah Beach Road,

avant-garde labels such as Yohji Yamamoto, Martin Margiela, Commes des Garçons and others can be found at IF Boutique in Umm Suqeim, and then there's the second-hand markets and events such as the Dubai Flea Market and My Ex Wardrobe. Be prepared to rummage, and don't be afraid to hit the souqs and old markets to haggle over deluxe silk fabrics.

S*UCE
1ST FLOOR, FASHION SECTION,
DUBAI MALL,
DOWNTOWN BURJ DUBAI.
TEL: 04 339 9696

+

GROUND FLOOR, THE VILLAGE MALL,
JUMEIRAH BEACH ROAD.
TEL: 04 344 7270

+

1ST FLOOR, NEW EXTENSION,
MARINA MALL,
ABU DHABI.
TEL: 02 681 8650

MY EX WARDRODE
WWW.MYEXWARDROBE.COM

SYMPHONY BOUTIQUE
SYMPHONY, GROUND FLOOR FASHION
AVENUE, THE DUBAI MALL.
TEL: 04 330 8050

WEST L.A.
SUNSET MALL ON JUMEIRAH BEACH ROAD.
OPEN SAT-THURS FROM 10AM - 10PM
FRIDAYS FROM 1.30PM - 10PM

GARDEROBE
JUMEIRAH ROAD, UMM SUQEIM 1,
PO BOX 73561.
TEL: 04 394 2753

IF BOUTIQUE
26, UMM AL SHEIF RD.
TEL: 04 394 7260

HAVE YOU EVER SEEN AN OKAPI?

PHOTOGRAPHY: **BASILE MOOKHERJEE**

TEXT: **JON BANTHORPE**

I can't tell you what I expected to see on my first visit to a private oasis. Part of me was hoping for obvious signs of wealth, draped in a single tiger.

In reality I was expecting tents, plenty of cushions, perhaps a few low-lying structures.

I certainly wasn't expecting 40 hectares of land that is home to 700 animals, comprising 110 species in total.

The Al Bustan Zoological Centre, which was once a date farm, is dedicated to the promotion of education, conservation breeding and research of animals. There are 99 full-time staff, which include a full-time construction team and a highly qualified management team, taking care of all aspects of the zoo and its residents, many of which are on the World Conservation Union (IUCN)Red List of Threatened Species.

Whilst touring in golf buggies, we met almost all the zoo's residents, ranging from indigenous goats to rhinos on a sabbatical from the San Fransisco Zoo. They has been flown over without needing to be sedated. Oh, and the Okapi, they are from the Congo, they were once referred to as the African unicorn and when you stroke them, they feel like velvet.

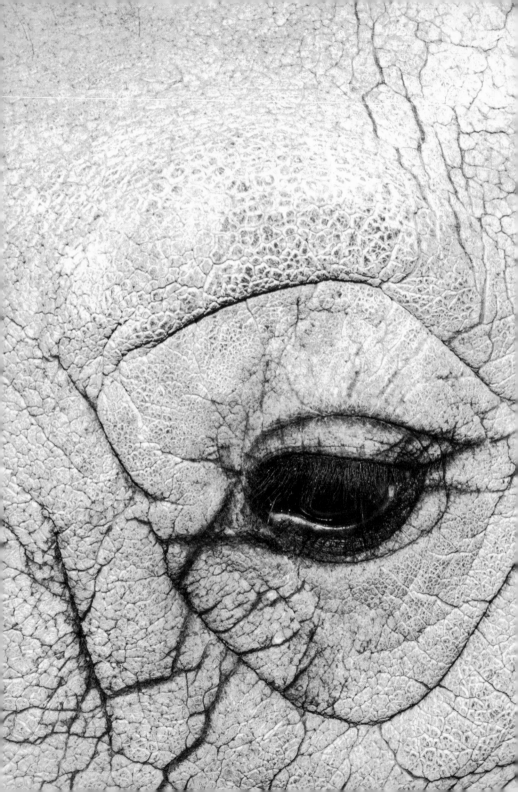

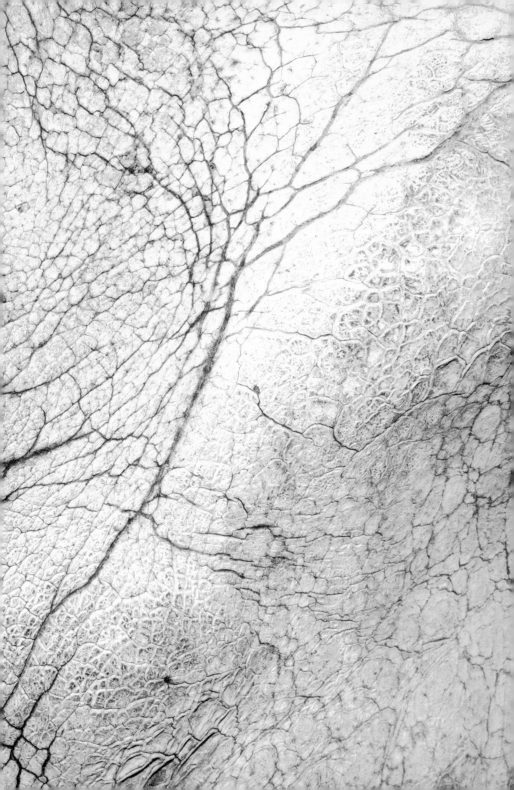

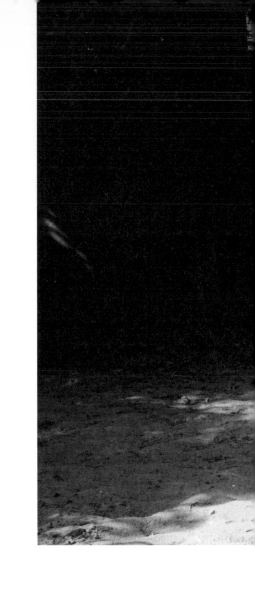

EAT, DRINK AND
BE MESSY

TEXT: **ELIOT BEER**

Visitors to Dubai split into two camps when the word 'brunch' is mentioned: the first either show no reaction, or look confused at why so apparently straight-forward an activity is such a big deal, the second camp look up with a gleam in their eye. Be worried of the second camp, for they know, or think they know, what's in store for them.

The basic concept of a long, boozy breakfast/lunch on Friday afternoons is straightforward - but as Dubai boomed, the brunches boomed along with it, and began to compete on size, spread and lavishness. By 2008, the number of brunches was into the triple figures, and the institution was hitting the headlines for all of the wrong reasons.

Like many long-term Dubai residents, I came to see the idea of regular brunches as a bit passé - not to mention expensive. When I did go out for brunch, it was generally to one of the more subdued affairs, such as the Glasshouse brunch in the Hilton Dubai Creek, or one with something a bit special, like the fresh and bountiful seafood at Wheeler's of St James in DIFC. But occasionally, visitors would show up and express a desire to go to a brunch - "a real brunch!" And so, with a sigh and some grumbling - and, perhaps, a quiet gleam in my own eye - I would acquiesce, and set out on the long hard road to gluttonous oblivion.

My first brunch experience was not especially large, lavish or decadent, being as it was at Waxy O'Connor's, one of Dubai's less-salubrious institutions, just before Christmas in 2005. Being new to Dubai, and not yet understanding its ways, I got there early - that is to say, on time - and spent an uncomfortable hour or so on my own at a table, nursing a Coke and trying to avoid the eye of the skinny, heavily-tattooed young man in the style of vest vulgarly known as 'wife-beater', who kept looking in my direction and winking at me. Fortunately, my companions turned up shortly after this, and I inaugurated my first Dubai brunch experience by staying in one place for almost the whole day and getting quite inebriated in the company of such questionable people as disgraced journalists and other journalists, as was the custom at the time.

My second venture was at the other end of the scale from Waxy's - the Yalumba brunch at Le Meridien Hotel in Garhoud, known for being one of the few brunches with free-flowing champagne at the time, a feature which should tell you most of what you need to know about the tone of the event. The rest of what you need to know is the laughing, shrieking presence of twenty-something girls with inflatable aquatic toys, frolicking in the shallow end of the hotel pool, and the overfed, braying thirty-something men with lobster complexions and crippling inferiority complexes. Ah, the happy memories.

Between then and the time I left Dubai some eight years later, I averaged two or so brunches a year, generally for special occasions, and once when I had one of those group discount voucher deals (pro-tip: discounted brunches are not as much fun. Damned if I know why, but it's true). Some have been delightful - the Glasshouse remains my favourite - some have been excruciating, and a few have been outright mistakes.

The one that sticks in my mind as the most quintessentially *brunchy* brunch of them all was for a friend's birthday at the Dusit Thani Hotel on Sheikh Zayed road. The host - known universally as 'Cue-ball' because that's what his head looked like - had gathered together in excess of 50 people for his birthday bash, and they were all out for a good time. My mind has suppressed much of what happened next, but I do have some clear flashes... a mutual friend, a well-built young woman, greeting me in the lobby by literally jumping into my arms... the shrieking, flailing trips to the outer reaches of the buffet... the mysterious disappearance of a third of the group mere minutes before the bill arrived... the establishment of a new base-camp at the bar next door to the restaurant... hiding behind the curtains... the open weeping...

I can't say I *enjoyed* it, exactly, but that brunch provided a handy benchmark against which all others can be measured. To date, nothing has topped more than 0.5 Dusits - but we can live in hope.

In the course of my various brunches over the years, I have made a number of mistakes, some of which now make me wince with shame. My lamentable timekeeping (see above), the times I have tried to combine unsuitable mealstuffs such as luminous orange curry and roast-beef-with-trimmings on a single plate, and (oh god) the time I failed to realise I had opted for the champagne option, and thus abstained throughout the brunch, only to pay the full whack at the end - such memories sometimes cause me to wake at night, sweating and staring wide-eyed.

In the spirit of education, then, I have assembled a few tips to allow you to make the most of your Dubai brunch. If you can follow these, then you may be reasonably assured of a satisfying yet not disastrous brunch experience:

1. Preparation begins the night before. While this may seem counterintuitive, turning up to a brunch while hung over puts you in a much more favourable frame of mind. Speaking from experience, there's little worse than turning up bright-eyed and bushy-tailed to a brunch, then attempting to get stuck in to rich food and free-flowing champers.

2. Pick your crowd. There are occasions when it is acceptable to dine alone: brunch is not one of them. Couples are also ill-advised - in fact, any party numbering less than six is asking for a dull time. Make sure your group is balanced internally as well - uneven gender splits are not necessarily a problem, but if you must include a boring person in your booking, make sure there's another Tedious Tim to keep them company and stop them inflicting themselves on the rest of the party.

3. Salads are for losers. Dubai brunches are where diets go to die - and if everyone is not on board with this, then you have a problem.

4. Lots of small plates. At most brunches, with the exception of a la carte affairs such as the Glasshouse, there's no limit to the number of times you can visit the buffet, except for your capacity - and possibly your shame. So don't try to overload your plate on the first visit with eight different foodstuffs - at best it becomes a gloopy mess and at worst it can end up being an all-too-accurate depiction of the aftermath of the brunch. Instead, get smaller, more coherent selections - and don't be afraid to go back for more if you find something you particularly like. Some people advocate trying to max out on the high-value dishes such as oysters or prime steak - but I'd say it's better to focus on what you enjoy.

5. Get strategic. When you get to your brunch, figure out if you're in this for the long haul, or if you're going for the sprint finish - this lets you set your pace of consumption. Balance is the key - especially at events like the JW Marriott's 12-hour brunch, where a slow and steady pace of grazing and sipping will see you through to midnight.

6. Sweet talk the staff. If you're feeling really ambitious, try tipping at the start of the brunch - I always wanted to try this at the Double Decker brunch at the Al Murooj Rotana - possibly the cheapest free-flowing drinks brunch in Dubai, with little else to recommend it - where I got the feeling the staff were under instructions to go slow on the *drinkies*, for the sake of the profit margins. If you try this out, do let me know how you got on...

7. Expect things to get messy. There have been brunches which passed off without incident, where all involved got up from the table sharply at 4pm, nodded smartly to each other, and went on their separate ways - but guess what: no-one talked about them the next day. (A friend likes to tell the story of the time he went to **Saffron** at Atlantis, at the behest of someone else, with the promise of disgraceful goings-on. By 4 o'clock my friend complained to his host that he hadn't seen a single fight yet - whereupon a table went over with a crash, and a weeping girlfriend started shouting "leave it Darren, he's not worth it!" Thus was balance restored). However, there's good mess and there's bad mess, so take some precautions to optimise the ratio. I strongly suggest paying your bill at the start of the brunch, especially in a large group - this removes any pressure at the end, and allows everyone to stagger off at the end without consequence. Also make sure to leave your passport and any truly essential items at home - some Dubaians go so far as to have a cheap 'brunch' phone, such is the rate of loss.

With that said, good luck - and good brunching.

BRUNCH DESTINATIONS:

WAXY O'CONNOR'S
ASCOT HOTEL, KHALID BIN WALEED RD.
TEL: 04 352 0900

DOUBLE DECKER
AL MUROOJ ROTANA, AL SAFFA ST.
TEL: 04 321 1111

GLASSHOUSE
HILTON DUBAI CREEK, BANIYAS ST.
TEL: 04 227 1111

DUSIT THANI
SHEIKH ZAYED RD.
TEL: 04 343 3333

YALUMBA
LE MERIDIEN DUBAI, AIRPORT RD.
TEL: 04 217 0000

SAFFRON
ATLANTIS THE PALM, CRESCENT RD.
TEL: 04 426 2626

LEISURELAND

TEXT & PHOTOGRAPHY: **HIND MEZAINA**

I'm always asked what was it like growing up in Dubai in the seventies and eighties. Where did I hang out with my friends? What did we do? Many (sadly) still assume there was nothing here in Dubai before the 2000s. It's as if Dubai the way we know it popped up out of nowhere. My childhood and teenage years were like growing up in any average small town. We used to hang out at each other's houses, watching TV and movies, or splashing about in the pool. We also went to the beach.

During my teen years, we hung out at the Al Ghurair Centre, one of the handful of malls/shopping centres in Dubai at the time. We also hung out on Al Diyafah Street (known today as 2nd December Street), where I'd buy music and rent movies from Disco 2000, grab a burger at Hardee's or a pizza at Pizza Hut. If we felt extravagant or had something to celebrate we'd go to Mini Chinese.
Many of these places are still around, but some have relocated or gone through a name change.

One place that hasn't changed much and is a spot of nostalgia for anyone that lived or grew up in Dubai in the 1980s is Al Nasr Leisureland. It's a place like no other in Dubai. You step in there and it's like time stood still. Not much has changed since it opened in 1979. It's a family friendly complex with sports facilities, including a very large swimming pool that had slides and waves. But during my childhood, I used to spend time in the Luna Park, playing on the

banana swings and pineapple slides and the bumper cars. I also hung out at the arcade; table ice hockey was a particular favourite game. The candy shop, which I remember was very pink and yellow, was also frequented many times.

Al Nasr Leisureland's logo included a penguin, which I guess was to promote the fact that it also had an ice rink. Although I was never good at skating, balancing myself was never my strongest point; I always loved the annual ice rink shows. They were quite extravagant affairs.

In the 1990s, my experience of the place changed, where I'd go to the bowling alley with friends and infrequent visits to the Lodge (a night club, where almost everyone in Dubai would end up on weekends). Yes, Al Nasr complex really had something for everyone.

But the biggest gem in that complex was Al Nasr Cinema. The first film I saw was in that cinema, I watched *Gandhi* in 1982, the year it was released. My school took us to the cinema; it was an educational trip. I will never forget the feeling I had when we walked into the middle aisle and I looked up at the giant screen. Think that's when my love of cinema started.

For most of the 1980s, the cinema showed Bollywood films and it was only in the 1990s that we started getting Hollywood blockbusters hitting our shores. (Otherwise, my movie viewing depended on renting pirated video cassettes from Disco 2000 on Al Diyafah Street).

Al Nasr Cinema only had one screen. Action films were big. I got to see most of the Van Damme, Schwarzenegger and Stallone movies. At the time, my taste in films was less selective compared to today. I went to watch everything – just for the joy of being in a cinema. It was a gathering point, we'd mill around, talking about the film, sitting on one of the benches outside the cinema. You'd bump into people you know there. This is when Dubai still felt small, when you felt like you knew almost everyone in the city.

Even watching the movies felt like a community activity. The action films in particular saw us cheer loudly when the bad guys got killed off, or boo at lame scenes. This was before I took cinema etiquette seriously. But hey, we were all guilty at the time. Was it the novelty of being in the cinema? But I've also had my fair share of shhing people when I was watching a serious film. The film snob in me wouldn't accept any talking or joking during a serious film.

When I was serious about watching a film, nothing would get in the way. I recall standing in line with a friend amongst kids on the opening night of *The Lion King* on a Friday evening. Think we were the only two adults trying to fight our way amongst kids. Imagine, I wanted to make sure I got in to get good seats before the kids. I cringe at the thought of how awful or obnoxious we must have appeared.

Film timings weren't reliable, as sometimes we'd have to wait for the reel to be transported from one cinema to another. How quaint.

Aladdin, The Bodyguard, Dances with Wolves, The English Patient, A Few Good Men, Forrest Gump, Jerry Maguire, Philadelphia, Seven, Shawshank Redemption, A Thin Red Line, Titanic, Toy Story, Twelve Monkeys, The Usual Suspects are some of the of films I remember watching there.

Around the mid to late 1990s, new, bigger, shinier multiplex cinemas started opening up in the new malls across the city. Al Nasr Cinema was no longer cool. It was ageing and not keeping up with the times or the technology.

Eventually Al Nasr Cinema stopped showing Hollywood blockbusters and went back to screening Bollywood movies, catering to a crowd that were still willing to go to Al Nasr Cinema. I wish I could say I remember the last film I saw there, but sadly I don't. Eventually, the building was abandoned, because even the Bollywood films and their audiences preferred the multiplexes.

I'd still drive past my favourite cinema whenever I was in Oud

Metha. But even though I was going to the other cinemas, it was not the same. I missed my first row balcony seats.

On 21st December 2008, I read this headline in Gulf News and my heart sank - *Massive fire erupts at Al Nasr Cinema in Dubai.* I regretted not visiting my favourite cinema after it was abandoned, not photographing it - to be able to share this part of Dubai's history.

Today, walking around Al Nasr Leisureland and the plot where the cinema was, which is still empty, everything looks much smaller than I remember, but I guess everything felt bigger when we were kids. I couldn't find the banana swings in the Luna Park, but the large fruit shaped rides were still there. I know if I take my young nephews to play there, they will mock me and describe it as too childish. Today's kids are so much more sophisticated.

There are more restaurants in Al Nasr Leisureland than I remember, the arcade hardly looks used, but the place had people using the sports facilities, including the bowling alley. A favourite with the drinkers in Dubai as it is one of the few places licensed to serve alcohol, the Lodge has been changed to Chi at the Lodge. It's no longer the meeting point for everyone on a weekend night like the old days. Next to it is a Goan club, Viva Goa, that has more character.

The penguin is still there. What an odd, yet delightful choice for a mascot/logo in Dubai. The main sign outside looks worn out. Could it possibly be the same one from 1979? I wouldn't be surprised if it is, and I'm glad it looks worn out. It's aged; it shows it has history, just like the place itself.

It's very easy to fall into the nostalgic trap when living in Dubai, the here and now never seems to be good enough. I along with many people I know miss the old days, the simpler days. For this story, I looked up Al Nasr Leisureland online. It never occurred to me that a website even existed. And there it was, the one line that captured the spirit of the place - *Discover the many pleasures of leisure.*

TALKING PATTERN

TEXT + ILLUSTRATION: **AZIZA IQBAL**

There is nothing more daunting to me than using words, instead of shapes and colours, to articulate my thoughts; to describe moments or places; or just to fill a page. I'm quite sure that my interpretation of Dubai as a pattern will say more than what I write.

I've always had a passion for Islamic art and geometry, and possibly the constant reverence to the art form has driven me to instinctively identify patterns and grids everywhere. Patterns, whether geometric, biomorphic or abstract, are almost like narrative for the discerning eye, ones that I'm always trying to break down; where they start, where they end, symmetries, rotations, consistencies, directions, vocabularies.

To speak Dubai, the city of glossy skyscrapers and *barjeels*[1], mind-bending highways and sand dunes, I found a captivating language in her heritage: the tradition of *Al Sadu* weaving. Practiced by Bedouins in the gulf for centuries, the traditional art in this nomadic region was focused on textiles - carpets, tents, horse and camel gear, furnishings - things that are easy to do on the move and at the same time, beautifully decorative and expressive. Using wool and natural dyes weaving was done exclusively by the womenfolk, and it was as much a social enterprise as a vocational one. And as with most traditional handicrafts, skills were passed on from the elders to the youth.

1. TRADITIONAL WIND TOWERS.

When I started this illustration, my primary aim was to do justice to the craft without making a factual copy. I needed to learn the essence of Emirati *Sadu* patterns. Whether I'm creating patterns or studying them, my process is just as haphazard as it is intensive, but I make sure my research is meticulous and organised, involving hours of looking at examples, searching for the reliable and geographically authentic.

Wherever Bedouins lived, Bedouins wove beautiful textiles, from Morocco to Iraq. What was distinct about the indigenous ones? The patterns are anything but arbitrary; narrow bands of geometric designs house a sequence of motifs, the typical *Sadu* design of distinctly simple geometry used to create a variety of shapes with associated symbolism and meaning, typically in white, black and red. Motifs are transformed by symmetry and repetition to generate a series of complex patterns that are woven into stories. Each tribe even has its own special markers, and *Sadu* styles vary across the Gulf.

Like the rest of the world, technology and modern living are driving many traditional crafts to extinction, but there are a few organisations in the Emirates, such as *Sougha*[1], encouraging artisans and bridging the gaps.

My approach was to focus on the actual weave of a *Sadu* piece. I used a series of small thread forms to put the full pattern together, trying in my own untrained way to see a design come together, knot by knot, perhaps as a real weaver would. A sense of parallel lines was my first impression from the traditional woven patterns, and this appealed to me as an apt representation of Dubai and her skyline. I wanted to create a pattern expressing not just her vertical-ness, but also her complexity and diversity.

1. SOUGHA IS AN INITIATIVE LAUNCHED BY KHALIFA FUND, IN PARTNERSHIP WITH SEVERAL GOVERNMENTAL ENTITIES, AIMED AT PRESERVING LOCAL HERITAGE THROUGH ARTISAN DEVELOPMENT, PRODUCT ADAPTATION AND OPPORTUNITY CREATION THROUGH MARKET ACCESS. SOUGHA TARGETS ALL CRAFTSMEN AND WOMEN WITHIN THE UAE.

REROUTE

OASIS OF CHARACTER

FRESH FISH AT THE BU QTAIR RESTAURANT

TEXT: **PAUL CASTLE**

"Does he actually know where he's going?" asks my wife, we're following our friend Mali in the car ahead of us, down the Jumeirah Beach Road. He keeps hesitating at right turns, only occasionally committing, then reversing course, back to the main drag.

"He said he'd been there before, a long time ago," says Adrianna from the back seat, beside her Kedar quips, "I'm guessing he was too young to drive for himself, at that time."

We're on the hunt for *Bu Qtair Cafeteria*, a somewhat legendary 'fish shack on the beach' in Dubai. And although we're hungry, the dozens of chain restaurants and fine dining establishments we pass give no temptation at all.

When my wife and I relocated from the USA to Dubai in mid 2008, we were eager for new experiences in what we expected to be a very unfamiliar country. Then we moved into our employer-provided apartment to find a mall directly across the street, with a McDonalds inside. The all-too-familiar had already preceded us to this 'exotic' destination.

However, as our home was in the Deira area of old Dubai we quickly found that the known was still greatly outnumbered by the unfamiliar. Soon, locally perennial restaurants like *Aroos Damascus, Al Bayt Al Bagdadi, Special Ostadi* and *Anapoorna* became common stops for interesting and affordable eats as we explored Dubai's older neighbourhoods, which we preferred over the malls and resorts for which the city is more widely noted.

Not long after our relocation, Twitter was unblocked by the UAE authorities and had a very positive effect on society in Dubai. Social circles expanded across previously daunting boundaries of nationality and occupation. Our collection of friends diversified greatly, including many like-minded sorts from all backgrounds and countries, whose idea of a great meal also bypassed Dubai's many lauded gourmet outlets.

It was a conversation on Twitter that started this particular quest. Adrianna - ever the bloodhound for venues with character - had asked if anybody knew where *Bu Qtair* was. Many of us had heard of it, but Mali had actually been there. Which is how ten of us ended up in this short parade of cars.

"On Jumeirah Beach, near the Burj Al Arab" was the usual general location given. But in an ever-growing city with no street addresses, the word 'near' becomes quite

a flexible term - if you can see a major landmark from a particular place, it must be "near" it, right? The memory of others is the primary atlas available, with varying results.

Block after block of walled villas give challenge to our hunt. In the couple of decades since *Bu Qtair* had originally opened, the Jumeirah area had grown up around it, morphing from a long stretch of sparsely populated dunes along the Arabian Gulf into a sprawling, upscale suburb. Finally, Mali turns down a street towards the beach and kept course. The scene changes dramatically as we reach our destination.

A portacabin on an otherwise vacant lot. This is our reward for diligence, only a sign above the door assuring us of our success. On either side, boats drawn up from the fisherman's village across the street appropriately frame the scene. And, yes, the *Burj Al Arab* Hotel is nearby, well less than 2 kilometres further down the beach.

The kitchen takes up most of the portacabin; from behind it, plastic tables and stools are dragged out by the staff to make a dining area of the bare lot in front. No menus - a promising sign in our book. Mali leads us in to the kitchen and we select our dinner from the mountain of freshly caught whole fish in the tray: *shari*, *pomfrett* and *hammour*, cleaned and slathered in chili and spices, South Indian style, and similarly prepared prawns. Once ordered it all goes to the back of the kitchen to be shallow fried.

Delivered to our table searing hot, steaming chunks of fish grabbed off the bone by hand with pieces of paratha flatbread as insulation, our meal is more than satisfying. Available to round out the meal are fish curry sauce, sliced cabbage, onions and lemons, and rice - simple, flavourful and fulfilling. There, in possibly the most relaxed setting in Dubai, we had found one of the most delicious meals any of us had ever enjoyed. The simplicity of the fare and the communal eating arrangement further elevated this as one of our most memorable outings together; our varied assemblage - American, Singaporean, Indian, Pakistani, Syrian and Philippine - had found the best of common ground.

We've returned many times to *Bu Qtair*, always with a large and diverse group of friends, and always heartily welcomed by Mr. Moosa behind the counter and Mr. Naser manning the tables. Perching on the flimsy stools, slipping bits of our meal to stray cats lurking under the tables, it's our preferred spot for birthdays, Christmas Eve and especially New Year's Eve, when we follow the meal with a stroll down to the beach to watch the massive fireworks displays sent up by the nearby resorts.

As the secret has gradually gotten out, *Bu Qtair's* popularity has proven to be quite broad. On any night the diners crowding the dimly lit scene are representative of Dubai's population; many are Indian, presumably many Keralites there to enjoy familiar cuisine, but a look around will reveal many Pakistani families and Philippine families too, with Levantine and Western expats evident. Emiratis are present as well, and many frequently stop on the street in front of the restaurant in their SUVs and honking their horn to draw out a waiter to get their order for takeaway, the Dubai equivalent of drive-through service.

Being such a consistently pleasant experience, *Bu Qtair* has received much attention in the last few years, garnering many articles in newspapers, blogs and magazines. It has been covered on TV as well, enjoying a visit from no less than Anthony Bourdain and his crew. Consequently, the hungry crowds have continued to swell, the line for ordering is ever longer, and it has become less uncommon to see tourists at *Bu Qtair*.

However, through all this *Bu Qtair* has changed little, in contrast to other old favourites around town that, if they have not simply gone out of business, have expanded, modernised and 'improved'. In a city that has been - and in many ways continues to be - a boomtown, permanence is a scarce commodity. Despite occasional tremors to the equilibrium, such as new signage exchanging 'Cafeteria' for 'Restaurant', or a waiter unexpectedly offering a plastic fork, *Bu Qtair* remains a shack near the beach, fronted by plastic tables, offering freshly-caught, freshly-cooked fish... and ample portions of lasting character.

MANY EXCELLENT HORSE-LIKE LADIES

PYONGYANG OKRYU-GWAN RESTAURANT

TEXT: **AGRI ISMAÏL**

"How do you spell it again? Is there a hyphen? I think I remember seeing a hyphen."

The reason that orthography and punctuation have become essential parts of our culinary journey is that our phones have, in the heart of Dubai's Al Rigga district, turned out to be about as useful as a bag of kittens trying to devise a comprehensive theory of cooper pair formation in unconventional superconductivity. As we debate the existence of the hyphen in the name and where it should be situated so we can - akin to a completed puzzle in Myst - magically unlock the path to the restaurant, my girlfriend and I walk slowly, necks craned over glass and aluminium phones that we're holding in front of us like *Ghostbusters* attempting to detect psycho-kinetic Energy. The maps on my phone have told me to go to Anheim, USA, while her phone is telling her that the restaurant she is looking for is in Beijing. In fact, there is a North Korean restaurant right here in Dubai, partly owned by the North Korean government. Or at least, so we're told. The one person we ask for directions looks at us as though we'd just asked him how to prove Fermat's last theorem using a spoon and piece of wood.

To be fair, the original Okryugwan in Pyongyang is known for its exclusivity. It is nearly impossible for someone who is not a member of the political elite to gain entry without a magical ticket (according to the internet), a ticket that you assume the country's leaders thought up after watching *Willy Wonka & The Chocolate Factory*. While the Dubai branch may not be difficult to get into, it is proving nigh impossible to actually locate.

Eventually we find it: a red, yellow and blue sign of saturated neon. In the window stands a young woman, dressed in a traditional Korean Chosan-ot (imagine, if you will, a dress made out of a giant wedding cake and Santa Claus' hat), smiling at us, giving us a wave to come in.

Well inside, the atmosphere changes for the better. A chorus of "annyeonghaseyo" washes over us as we are welcomed and given two pleather menus that helpfully say MENU on the cover. Even more helpfully, the dishes that are translated from the Korean into a near-poetic paste of nonsense purporting to be English (e.g. 'steamed nutritious koryo / Insam mash beef') are accompanied by images so that when one of the waitresses comes to take our order, we can simply point and grunt.

But before we order, we sit in hushed reverence at this most bizarre institution. This branch exists, like those in China, mainly to be able to send back US dollars to a country in desperate need of foreign currency. The waitresses, all dressed in blue polka-dot dresses and red shoes, are uniformly beautiful and have allegedly undergone double eyelid surgery - a supposed prerequisite for having the prestigious job of being a waitress at one of these restaurants. When asked if they like Dubai, they all smile politely. "North Korea Nicer."

We start to wonder what their life is actually like. One of the Beijing branches was closed after one of the waitresses tried to abscond (they are not allowed to go outside unaccompanied) and the entire staff was sent back to North Korea in order to, presumably, be given ice cream and catch up on the North Korean equivalent to *Breaking Bad*. We find that the human ability to empathise has its limits: we know nothing about North Korea outside of a vague idea that it is hell on earth.

The television that is showing a looped video of some fish has had the Samsung logo scratched off, and yet there is a refrigerator by the entrance filled with soda that has Coca-Cola written all over it. There may not - surprisingly - be any photos of the holy trinity of Kims but for the first time I understand the concept of the 'Eternal Chairman' - their presence looms even though they're not here.

To talk of the food amidst this scenario is almost beside the point. It so happens, however, that the food is great: the cold noodles the restaurant is famed for are far tastier than the unappetising moniker would lead you to believe, the kimchi has just the right sour tang and the raw meat that is brought to the table to be grilled is enough to feed a legion. If there wasn't a sign that said that photography was not allowed hanging above my head - and my fear of what a North Korean establishment would do if I disobeyed orders - the spread would be worthy of an Instagram.

The waitresses come out of what I later find out are private karaoke rooms for the regular patrons, now dressed as porcelain geishas. They begin to sing a Korean song that sounds eerily like the theme to the Teletubbies. My girlfriend and I look at each other while all around us beautiful North Korean women twirl saying "eh-oh". Only the woman dressed as a cake isn't dancing: she's by the window sill, looking out, waving at anyone who passes by.

AL MAKTOUM ROAD, DEIRA.
TEL: 04 298 1589
TIMES: OPEN DAILY 10.30AM-MIDNIGHT
CREDIT CARDS ACCEPTED: YES

PERFECT COOL

TEXT: **LAYLA MAGHRIBI**

PHOTOGRAPHER: **KIMBERLEY SIWIEC**

It took many weekends of me and my Dubai friends' failed insistence that we 'do something different and outdoorsy' before we actually set off to explore what lies beyond Dubai's city skyline.

Expats in Dubai love to boast to those in their home countries (often wet and windy) of how the all-year sun, sea and seemingly endless swathes of desert make for a gorgeously active outdoor lifestyle. Truth is that for about six months of the year the only thing frying outside is your skin.

For most of the bankers, accountants, journalists (like myself), public relations or any other white-collar worker bees here we're more used to buzzing from the office to one hot, new art gallery or yet another new, hip bar opening. It may not read of something to pity but this lifestyle doesn't lend itself much to 'stopping to smell the flowers' (despite the fact that Dubai houses the world's largest Miracle flower garden).

But if you muster up a good group, some 4x4s and smidge of organisation, then it is worth trying the Hatta wadis, (also known as Hatta Pools). Wadis is the Arabic name for valleys. They are generally dry except after rain, but visits should be avoided during rain. Although very intermittent, sudden onsets of heavy rains - known as flash floods - can be very dangerous and have claimed some lives.

Hatta is a sheikhdom in an exclave of the Emirate of Dubai. Its capital, also named Hatta, includes a reconstructed heritage village with two prominent military towers built in the 18th century and some 30 houses made of silt and clay. Although technically in the UAE you will need your passports to hand because a military checkpoint sits at the border of a swathe of land called the Buraimi in Oman, before you reach Hatta. After about 120km of highway and generic roundabouts you approach the arid, jagged brownie-grey Al-Hajjar Mountains, some of which reach 1,300 metres, making them all the more striking for their seemingly random emergence out of the flat desert.

Hatta's high elevation makes for a milder climate and, as a result, is a popular local vacationing spot. After some

10km of exciting and steep twists on the slim mountain dual carriageway (an excitement tempered by the numerous, long black tire marks on the roads), you exit onto rough terrain.

It takes about 150 km, less than two hours, to drive out of the city centre to get to the wadis. Although outdoorsy discoveries have been a by-product of my job - including the above-mentioned Miracle Garden, a dairy farm, endangered animals retreat and other equally atypical desert places - none of these have been part of my own personal down-time, so it was with great pleasure that I merrily took my 4x4 Jeep to see some actual off-road action for the first time that year.

Reaching the spot, we parked and walked a few hundred metres down the mountain and arrived at the natural spring gorges some ten metres below a crevice. We had been guided there by one of our friend's Dads - a Dubai resident of over 30 years - who used to take his children to the Hatta wadis for picnics and dips in the crystalline pools when the children were very little. Back then, when his daughter was about 5 years old, she'd just fearlessly fling herself into the water. Fast forward 20-something years and she and her 10-strong entourage could barely muster the courage to peer over these edges (now seemingly 'cliffs' to us).

The embarrassment of our murmurings that the water surely wasn't deep enough to jump into was only amplified when the father - twice our age - jumped in instantly to assuage our fears. Mildly horrified, we realised that there was no turning back now that the 60 year old who - thanks to shunning the 20 to 30-something Dubai lifestyle - looked fitter than all of us.

We all huddled to assess the now transparent water that filled the gorge. With only a ten-metre gap between the opposite sides of these mountain faces, the gap is wide enough to jump into like a pencil, but just short of running or flipping into (unless, like one of the guys in our group, you do a backflip into it to impress a girl).

Not all of us were so emboldened. One guy stood like a statue, toes curled around the edge, eyes fixed down below. Encouraged - or embarrassed - by the din of us cheering him on he would take a few steps back like a catapult only to halt once more at the edge to a chorus of groans.

Despite the seeming desolateness of the place, it is in fact a great draw for many locals, tourists and expats, especially those from the subcontinent who come for a relatively cheap day-trip away from the hustle and grind of working in the city. On weekends the area is packed with streams of 4x4s and pick-up trucks unloading blankets, folded chairs and huge picnic spreads. The fact that most of them don't swim isn't a deterrent. There are always 'crazy' folk like us who rock up in our shorts and bikinis to jump in and out of the wadis like yo-yos.

It was probably this cacophony of cheery jeering that drew the attention of some of the Sub Continental day-trippers, unsuitably clad for wadi-jumping in shalwars and kameeses, who had surreptitiously appeared and silently inserted themselves into our playful scene to watch.

By the time my turn came to jump, we had amassed an audience. Squirming with trepidation against the rocks, the sounds of my friends sniggering below made me

look up to find two-dozen pairs of male eyes, watching me from the opposite cliff-side. Where there was fear of potential paraplegia for, there was now performance anxiety to contend with.

Eventually, a friend held my hand and in we jumped, into the beautiful and perfect temperature water. Once we had all broken our initial fear barriers there was no stopping us, splashing ourselves in and working our way out over slippery rocks to do our 'tricks' for our viewers all over again. The single jumps, the backflips, the group-handhold-while-singing-happy birthday jump (good for generic e-cards we decided). The rush of joy and energy beamed across all our faces, filling us city-slickers with child-like enthusiasm. Bringing out the goofy and unabashed inner child was exactly what most of realised we needed.

For many of us struggling with the ever-present, low-level stresses of city life, the act of jumping was a total release of control.

Some described the moments of falling as completely 'dream-like'; the sensation of being immersed in the fresh water pools being one of great freedom - particularly for those otherwise constrained to desks and chairs all week. In a city with constant whishing and whooshing on six-lane highways, surrounded by 100-metre wide billboards, Hatta was a humbling and peaceful experience.

Despite dodging kamikaze drivers on the highway back and hitting the peak Friday night traffic you will find yourself still buzzing on a high. That is not to say we didn't take our energised selves out for several hours of dancing later that same evening. Because, after all, that's the real coolness of Dubai - being able to look out across a mountainous desert in the morning and then go dancing in a vibrant bar, in the balmy night of the city.

LOST IN AL QUOZ

TEXT: **DANNA LORCH**

There is no point wearing nice shoes, especially black, velvet smoking slippers. They will only get dusty and torn. Don't even try heels. You'll just sink into the sand up to your pretty ankles. Unless you have a Mercedes SUV with a father-like driver dressed in a dinner jacket that calls you, 'Madame' and won't let you tiptoe further than the car to the gallery door. But then, your spontaneity would be smothered.

You'll need a good map. You can't walk here from any metro station. Cab drivers won't know this place. Tell them you're going to Al Quoz and they will mutter "crazy tourist" and try to reroute you to a *souk* selling plastic replicas of the *Burj Khalifa*. You will pass car repair shops, a boxing club and a Pakistani cafeteria. Industrial is the adjective that will come to mind.

Your driver probably lives nearby, but not in this part of the district where young professionals go to feel countercultural. The other Al Quoz—just 5 minutes away - where thousands of labourers and workers bunk in camps built of beige concrete. If you cruised slow enough on a Friday night to peek in those windows you'd have seen bunk beds, laundry lines, fluorescent overhead lights and smudged stairwells. You might have stopped at a red light and watched as a crowd 200-strong, many holding hands and laughing into their Nokia phones, crossed the intersection towards Al Quoz Mall.

If you begin to hug your elbows and cross your legs, anxiously wondering if the driver is kidnapping you and taking you to an abandoned area of town where you will be tied up and frozen in a meat locker to be found, rescued and defrosted by no one ever, then you are in the right place. The first time I took my husband here we were still newlyweds and he turned to me as though I were a masked stranger to ask, "Are you taking me here to have me whacked by the mob?" Actually I was taking him to an art night at Alserkal Avenue where we binged on a photograph by a Syrian artist the way other people binge on couture. The photograph was not mass-produced in a sweatshop in China and I did not have to be tall, svelte and skinny to own it.

Alserkal Avenue is poorly marked. When you find it at last you feel as though you have unearthed a secret. The building is the colour of the Atlantic Ocean on a melancholy winter's morning. It once housed a marble factory owned by the Alserkal family, an Emirati family known for its patronage of the arts. A few galleries opened spaces here five years ago and the place grew organically until more than 20 warehouses were renovated and turned into galleries. Step into a white cube and suddenly you're in Iran, Pakistan or France. I can hear the purr of cranes beyond, the bird song of Dubai - Alserkal is currently doubling in size. I step through the gates

and admire the street art on the wall. Graffiti is still officially illegal in Dubai, but in the last year it has started to appear on private buildings.

I turn right and pass through a steel door into **Salsali Private Museum**. The wall in front of me blinks with a neon sign that reads alternately, "THIS IS A MUSEUM! THIS IS NOT A MUSEUM!" The floor is polished concrete. The air is blindingly cool. It is so quiet inside that for a split second I feel as though I shouldn't be here. I used to feel that way every moment when I first came to Dubai two years ago. Like I didn't belong. Like everyone could tell that my clothes were cheap, my cuticles were ragged and I wasn't Arab. I was surrounded by women in silk cocktail dresses everywhere I went, all of them in stilettos with potent smiles and colossal diamond rings, asking me what I do and who I know, then smiling right through me. Until I came here. Slipped through this door into a place that could not be labelled. "THIS IS A MUSEUM! THIS IS NOT A MUSEUM!" **Salsali** is the first private museum in the region. Entirely free, open long hours even in summer, and containing a rotating collection of private work and commissions.

I leave **Salsali** and totter down the uneven alley towards the other galleries. The artists from **Ayyam Gallery** are chain smoking on wooden benches, their backs pushed against the building, sunning themselves like cats while shooting espresso from chipped mugs. Their uniform is skinny black jeans, glasses and t-shirts. Many of them have come to Dubai for artistic freedom from places in the region where there is none. **Ayyam** is known for incubating emerging artists from Syria and it is not unusual to see high-end work beside an experimental abstract by a young unknown.

Back in the alleyway, I try the door to **Lawrie Shabibi** but find it locked. They are away at a prestigious art fair in Europe. Too bad! The owners are great storytellers and have witnessed Dubai's transformation into an art market. I open an unmarked door to find four guys in grey *shalwar khameez*[1] sanding wood in a workshop.

This is not a gallery, Madame!

I head to the back of the compound, past the trash dumpsters to visit **Grey Noise**, a gallery transplanted from Lahore that is usually filled with androgynous hipsters in thick-rimmed glasses making bluntly critical comments. The work is experimental. Sometimes I don't understand the installations but pretend to. Other times I feel so connected to a show that I beg to make a pallet for myself on the floor so I'd never have to leave.

Shading my skin from the sun with a red umbrella, I leave Alserkal and walk through the dust to Street 6 behind. The skeleton of a dhow sits outside a salmon coloured building with out of date windows. A sign reads '**Courtyard**'. I wander inside and find myself in what looks like a movie set of an abandoned Tuscan village. I trip on the cobblestone.

Somewhere a wind chime hums like a ghost. Random furniture and design stores are upstairs. For a moment I wish I were a turn of the century housewife with an hourglass figure scrubbing laundry in a

1. A TRADITIONAL DRESS FROM SOUTH AND CENTRAL ASIA, WORN BY BOTH MEN AND WOMEN.

wooden bucket waiting for my husband to return from battle, our children chasing one another through the village like a litter of scrappy pups.

Next door is **Limetree Café**, which is packed with gallerists at lunch—all of them air kissing on the cheeks and dressed in black, sipping date smoothies, cluttering the tables with Moleskine notebooks and press release drafts. Sometimes it's impossible not to eavesdrop.

Back on Street 6, I walk a few metres to **The Third Line**. The upstairs space under the eaves has introduced me to some of my favourite emerging artists. It has a bench that encourages lingering. Once I was invited into the stock room for a mug of builder's tea. I looked wistfully at the rows of paintings packed away in wooden coffins waiting to be sent to their final resting places.

There are days that I visit Al Quoz and am ignored or brushed off. I'm still growing into my role as a critical writer. The art community here is a mother without a maternal instinct. She is capable of holding grudges but her complexity is more alluring than a pearl diver's treasure. I am her rebellious teenage daughter, unafraid to talk back, to grow taller with dew on my cheeks, to claim my own spirit.

FRIDAY RITUAL

TEXT: **HAJER ALMOSLEH**

PHOTOGRAPHY: **REEM FALAKNAZ**

I live in a city that is a continent of sand and light and sun-kissed memories. To cross from one side of the continent to another, I could walk, run, hop on a bus, wave down a taxi, ride the metro, or cross on a wooden Abra, sitting next to strangers who call me sister. Whenever I can, I opt for the latter.

To get to the Abra from Bur Dubai, I walk through Bastakiya, the historic area of Dubai which hosts Sikka Art Fair every year, and beckons with stories tucked behind the low roofs and warm construction, reminiscent of a past so close, a history which refuses to be dwarfed by skyscrapers and world records. Go to the Old Souk in midday and it will make you forget the futuristic city rising all around it. Go to it at night and feel the city come to its knees to kiss its sinewy hand.

It is midday on Friday. The mosques are full and I pass the clean, white-washed mosque in Bastakiya. Its entrance is littered with men's shoes and slippers. Littered but not untidy. My nose picks up the smell of amber. On my way to the Old Souk, my Friday ritual, I always pass by this mini paradise, and I'm aroused by the whiteness inside, the sight of men rising and bending, the uniformity of their prostrate bodies in front of me.

It is still early October, the humidity in the air and the relentless sun refuse to make way to breeze. Soon enough, when the weather is less harsh, the men will be praying outside.

Bastakiya and the Old Souk face each other, on different banks of the Creek. Bastakiya has always been the female in my mind and the Old Souk the slightly older male poet, weaving epics about her beauty, inscribing them on pennants, infusing them with spice and myrrh, nailing them to the walls of his heart, daily.

It costs only a dirham to cross the creek on the Abra. Today, I am the only woman on the Abra, surrounded by Indian, Pakistani and Afghani men who gaze at me and pretend they're looking in the other direction. The man on my right is carrying a plastic bag. I can smell the mouthwatering spices of biryani and samosas. Around us is the smell of fish and deep waters.

"Where are you from?" He asks.

"Palestine," I say, I'm impressed he doesn't mistake it for Pakistan, although he thinks I am Italian.

The guy on my left, in a *sharwal kameese* and a white skull hat, asks me my name.

"Hajer," I say.

"Ah, Hajerah!" he corrects me using the Urdu pronunciation of my name.

I don't carry a camera with me. I no longer do. I like to see the same sights, walk the same distance, get thrilled or jarred by it, rocked to my bones experiencing it anew. I like it when people at the Souk, who have seen me a myriad of times, and forgotten my face as soon as I left, think that I am there for the first time. Hymenoplasty of the brain, that's what I call it.

The man to my right, Ashok, offers me a samosa and I gladly accept. He is going to his friend's house, he tells me.It is less than seven minutes on the Abra and now we're on the other side of the creek. Ashok offers to walk with me.

"You don't have to, I know my way."

It is Ashok that I don't know. But I don't say that to him. He walks with me nonetheless.

"I live very close to here. You can be my guest one day," he offers.

"I also live here, Ashok," I tell him, he struggles to understand.

No, I am not a tourist. I've been calling Dubai home for the last seven years.

In this part of Dubai you find everything. One souk opens into another: **Al Souk Al Kabeer**, the **Gold Souk**, the **Old Souk**. You can find everything and see everyone. Here you find Pakistanis, Iranians, Afghanis and Africans, here you hear every language but you might not hear a word of Arabic.

I feel welcomed as I meander through the narrow lanes of the souk. I am constantly asked where I am from and invited to "come in". I walk out of a shop with a small bag of succulent golden raisins. The shopkeeper refuses to let me pay. "This is from my country," he says, he is Indian.

I squeeze my way through the throngs of tourists who emerge suddenly, groups descending from identical buses, flocking around polyglot tour guides who know the language the Euro speaks. Tourists who know what they want and those who just left their 5-star hotel rooms and are awestruck with this part of Dubai. The abundance of it all.

The stores are similar. Almost identical. I never cease to wonder how the workers distinguish one store from the other. Open burlap sacks full of dried lime, rose tea, sage, black tea and frankincense. At the entrance of one store, sticks of cinnamon stand like guards, deep brown, intact and majestic.

Aziz, the shop owner, expostulates on the benefits of cinnamon. I want to tuck a stick in my drawer or grind it and sprinkle it like fairy dust on my shawls.

"Do you have saffron?" I ask Aziz.

But of course he does. It's tucked inside a glass box in the store. You don't put saffron in burlap sacks. You protect it. It is more expensive than gold.

Aziz is proud of his saffron. He opens the glass box for me to inspect the precious reddish stigmas lying inside.

"This is half a kilo of saffron. It takes the size of a football field of saffron flowers to make one kilo of saffron," he tells me.

Today, Aziz invites me to go to Iran for saffron harvest.

"You are my guest in Iran," he says as he hands me his card. "Just get your visa. In two weeks I buy you a ticket and you go to my country and you take pictures and you write about saffron."

I smile and thank him. He reads in my smile a dismissal, and he is offended.

"I am serious," he says, "you come to my country."

I promise him to take him up on his word.

"What else do you want today?" He asks.

Cloves.

He runs his hands through the small, brown nails of cloves and invites me to do the same. I feel them tickle my palms and pass like murmurs between my fingers. My hands absorb their perfume.

I am asked to run my hands through a mound of cardamom, the third most expensive spice in the world, by weight. I am surrounded by the luxury of it. Aziz cracks one pod open, smells it and then starts chewing it. I do the same. When he talks, he smells of the mild Arabic coffee I had the night before, laced with cardamom and saffron.

In this section of the Souk, I am suddenly aware of the absence of harsh sounds. No cars honking, no cars speeding. It's calm. As though the aroma of spices has thickened the air around with its protective, reassuring rawness. The outside world, the fuming industrial commercial madness does not travel this deep.

Here your senses rework their priorities. You almost hear the songs of hands harvesting...harvesting...reaching for more.

Almost automatically, I close my eyes as I walk out of Aziz's store, deeper into the Souk.

Spice and perfume shops overlap each other. Smells inviting you to the courts of sultans and viziers. When I think of a story from Arabian nights, a big wooden gate opens and I'm ushered in, laced with *camphor* and *oud* and burning frankincense. The simple act of inquiring about perfumes scents the tongue. The thick pure oils dominating the shelves, one drop of dehan al oud, on the wrists, behind the ears. This is the smell of Friday. Of weddings. Of peaceful death. Of paradise.

"Lovers use it as an aphrodisiac," someone whispers next to me. A tourist who has done his research and is there to see the real product for himself.

There is a hunger for *Oud* within me. The scent of my mother's lap when she braided my hair. The day she hugged me goodbye, years ago, and I never saw her again. On my father's white *thoub* as he came home from the mosque.

It's the sensuous smell of veiled women.

In one store, sticks of *bukhoor*, like queens, carefully stretch on velvet lining. It comes from India, Cambodia, Malaysia. The shop keeper, Hasan, lifts a very small piece, the size of the tip of my finger, and lays it on top of burning coals in decorated incense burner, *mabkhara*. The smell is predominant. Powering, but not overpowering. The smoke weaves itself through of my hair.

There's a glass jar on the counter. It has a new homemade body scrub and Hasan sells it by the kilo. It is a combination of amongst other things oud, saffron and vanilla. Hasan tries to numerate them for me but his English doesn't help him. He puts a couple of drops on the back of my

hand. I scrub it and my hand feels soft and enchantingly delicious. I am tempted to lick it. The smell lasts on my hand even after I wash it much later.

I stop at **Aden Restaurant** for *Mandi*, *Madhbi* and Madghod before I take the Abra back to other side of the creek. I sit down cross-legged on the floor and eat the rice and lamb. There is cardamom. There is cinnamon.

It costs one dirham on the Abra. Every Friday I find myself falling in love with Dubai all over again. When you are on the Abra, you don't see the skyline of Dubai with its skyscrapers. You almost believe that they haven't been built yet. As the Abra starts moving to the opposite side of the creek, I see the twin Rolex towers to my left, not exactly skyscrapers, but definite reminders of time in every sense of the word.

Every week I leave the souk with something. This time, I leave with small bags of spices nestling comfortably in the bottom of my oversized bag, and with Aziz's invitation to go to his hometown in Iran in two weeks. I don't buy saffron. That I am going to pick in Iran.

HINDI LANE

TEXT + IMAGERY: **ALI TAHERI**

I was never meant to live in Dubai for as long as I have. My time and experience in the city was meant to catapult me towards 'greater' things, which I had imagined would provide me with a 'better' life. My negative attitude towards the glamour and façade obscured my relationship with my environment. With each day, I grew more determined to paddle my way through the Strait of Hormouz in hopes of finding an island in the Indian Ocean I could call mine. This perception no longer exists. And while I do maintain my ambitions of finding a greener home far away from the Persian Gulf someday, Dubai can be as charming as any cultured city in the world.

What I learned was that to truly experience the colourful adventures Dubai has on offer, one would have to treat it as any tourist would. The preservation of a routine life is a common practice amongst long-term residents of the city. To venture beyond the borders of extravagant norms and lifestyles is a rare custom, but I dared to step out of the shadows and into the colourful streets and alleyways bursting with values and cultures uncommon to many.

The **Old Souk** in Bur Dubai is where it all started. My mentor and I decided to collaborate and put together a short film with melancholic undertones. We scoured the uninhabited dark pathways of the old souk in the early hours, and by daybreak, we had filmed all that we needed. We settled by the creek and watched as life started anew. Our unimaginable thirst for some 'chai karak' (an Asian concoction of tea and milk, overdosed with sugar) led us into a narrow street that had seemingly just awoken from its humble slumber. We had stumbled upon 'Hindi Lane'.

Situated between Bur Dubai's Grand Mosque and the creek, the narrow lane is home to the only Hindu temple in the United Arab Emirates. Folklore tales claim that the temple was a gift from the late ruler of the UAE, Sheikh Zayed, to the Hindu and Sikh community residing in the country. And ever since its inauguration, the tiny street has been transformed into a little India not too far away from India. One could never imagine that a street so confined (it's so narrow that natural sunlight barely squeezes itself through at noon)

could maintain such dexterity and discipline. It takes three minutes to stroll through the high walls, but you would be forgiven for spending an entire morning engaging with all on offer.

The street has no beginning or end. Vibrant shades of red and orange clutter your east and west regardless of your polar position, and the echoes of wind chimes and Hindu hymns pulsate. Worshippers pace towards the temple in fashionable grace and you can't help but steer clear of their path. As I made my way towards the entrance of the temple, I noticed the shopkeepers filling plastic bags with jasmine, roses and other scented flowers to sell as tributes to the Gods. Bananas, sweets, milk cartons and other delicacies are also bunched up into little plastic bags and used as tribute. The whole process is systematic, and to my untrained eye, quite organised and faultless. What little breeze flows through the street carries with it the aroma of a thousand lit incense sticks. And as I hastily manoeuvred myself through the crowd, the heavenly scent interweaved with the odours of coconut oil and potent musk.

To enter the temple, I was obliged to take off my shoes and wear a bright orange head cover. I respectfully fell into line and followed others as they climbed the dozen wooden steps into the temple. Once inside, I helped myself to some tea before settling down to witness the worshippers pay their tributes as they prayed to their idol Gods. I watched in admiration as both the Sikhs and Hindus whispered pleasantries to one another on their way out.

Most of the street had willingly rid itself of the glittering chaos by the time I'd made my way out of the temple. The mothers with their curious children had retired back to their homes. The rest scattered for lunch or their bread winning commitments. I tip-toed my way back to the shoe rack, avoiding puddles of saliva. It was half past noon and it seemed that life had abruptly summoned itself into a transitory coma.

Before the market shut for the afternoon, I managed to browse through wares on display. I found everything one would need to turn their home into a mini temple. From multi-coloured prayer beads to large-sized intricate posters of Hindu Gods such as Shiva and Krishna. The shopkeepers must have sensed my indecisive behaviour. They released their curtains, locked the doors and vanished into the side streets.

I walked past a watchman (whose duty is to regulate the flow of human traffic during worshipping hours and to watch over the shops whilst others rested), and decided to call it a day. As I reached the end of the street, I noticed that one store still had its doors open. I walked in and greeted the old man behind the counter. As it turns out, the street comes to life at 5am till half past noon, and again from half past four till 10pm. He invited me in for a cup of 'chai karak' and shared his stories with me in what very little English he could speak. My clothes soaked up the aroma of his store and I left with memories of an afternoon spent in a city I never thought existed.

I also bought a few boxes of incense sticks.

CHABAB ANYONE?

TEXT + PHOTOGRAPHY: **HIND MEZAINA**

Emirati food in public spaces is strangely lacking. It's so easy to go out for Chinese, Italian or Indian, but the same can't be said when it comes to Emirati food.

I am always asked - what is Emirati food? I always reply that it's simple and basic food - rice, fish, meat are the main ingredients, with some of our dishes influenced from Iran and the Indian Subcontinent.

Unless you are invited to an Emirati house or wedding, or visit the **Sheikh Mohammed Centre for Cultural Understanding**, you may not get a chance to taste Emirati food. If you do, you are likely to encounter these dishes:

Harees - porridge-like dish of barley with meat/chicken, mostly popular during Ramadan and special occasions such as weddings.

Thareed/fareeth – thin, flat bread and lamb stew.

Machboos – a rice dish.

You won't find Arabic coffee, *sulaimani* tea or *chabab* (a pancake that can be served with eggs, cheese or date syrup) and *balaleet* (sweetened vermicelli) in any regular cafés here, whereas you will find cappuccino and croissants.

You won't find sweets like *luqeymat* (sweet dumplings) on the dessert menu. Whereas you are guaranteed to find the Egyptian dessert, *Um Ali*, included in

buffets at most hotels or non-specific restaurants that serve Arabic food.

I have always wondered why there is a lack of Emirati food on offer in public spaces. In a recent interview on CNN with Emirati chef Ali Ebdowa (Emirates Palace Hotel in Abu Dhabi), in which he was asked why there are so few Emirati restaurants, he cited the lack of Emirati chefs as the reason, as it is not deemed prestigious enough as a career.

I'm not convinced that's the only reason.

Emiratis are obsessed with international brands, even when it comes to food. Does it mean Emirati food isn't considered worthy enough to be a cuisine that can be cooked and served outside an Emirati home? I imagine many Emiratis would ask: why should I go out and eat Emirati food when I can have it at home?

Food always connects people and I personally think the lack of Emirati food across the city is one of the reasons why there's a 'locals' and 'expat' divide.

Shawarma stands are a dime a dozen, so why can't we find similar stands selling *chababs* and traditional coffee and tea?

The recent introduction of the camel burger, served in some of the touristy parts of Dubai, received a lot of publicity, with people trying it more for the novelty factor, rather than to taste and learn more about Emirati food.

Parts of Dubai populated by Emiratis already have a range of shops/places that serve Emirati food and sweets. It's the lack of these places in the rest of Dubai that is the issue. How to get the non-Emiratis engaged with Emirati food?

Emirati restaurants have begun to crop up, restaurants that don't look like your 'straight-out-of-a-guidebook' kind of place. They maintain the local touch, serve Emirati food and drinks, and are frequented by locals and expats alike. Below are a few worth visiting:

AL FANAR IN DUBAI FESTIVAL CITY, GARHOUD, OPENED A COUPLE OF YEARS AGO AND PROMOTES ITSELF AS A PLACE THAT SERVES AUTHENTIC EMIRATI FOOD. IT IS FILLED WITH INTERESTING MEMORABILIA THAT BELONG TO THE OWNER OF THE RESTAURANT.

BAIT 1971 ON THE BEACH FRONT IN JUMEIRAH HAS GAINED POPULARITY.

KLAYYA BAKERY AND SWEETS IS A CUTE CAFÉ IN BARSHA MALL THAT SERVES FRESH BREADS AND DELICIOUS KARAK TEA.

MAMA TANI IN TOWN CENTRE, JUMEIRAH, IS A RECENT ADDITION THAT HAS A SIMPLE MENU OF DIFFERENT TYPES OF KHAMEER (BREAD) THAT IS SERVED WITH A VARIETY OF FILLINGS. THEY ARE ALSO TRYING TO INFUSE TRADITIONAL SPICES INTO POPULAR DISHES.

NAUGHTY, NICE, SWEET DEXTER AND DRAGON

TEXT: **DANA DAJANI**
PHOTOGRAPHY: **NICK ZAJICEK**

Dubai still carries that 'new car smell' which has yet to be replaced by the smog of time, because this is new Dubai. A consumer heaven, rife with every foreign franchise you could ever desire. A place where even our nightlife is imported; with bars like Mahiki and Cirque du Soir, we are big fans of whatever the West is selling.

Years ago, before this was a city I called home, I made a habit of escaping the cold Chicago winters to visit family in Dubai. Upon every arrival I was awestruck at the growth, construction and industry. I went out to bars and clubs like Armani and 400. I gawked at the lifestyle of excess, a novelty experience, before returning to my modest studio apartment and hungry artist reality in America.

One winter night, an Indian friend of mine invited me on an adventure to explore Bur Dubai. I met with him, his Italian friend, and a girl from Belgium, and we embarked on our journey towards a very seedy hotel with an even seedier bar. The locale was a big change from the glitzy clubs I had been to in the previous weeks. I was told we were there for one reason only: to watch a live performance, the likes of which I did

not know existed in this town. From that night on, I was hooked.

After moving to Dubai, whenever I tired from the plastic programme, I organised a cultural evening in Bur Dubai. Dinner at a Greek restaurant, drinks at an Ethiopian Dance Hall, and on and on. My favourite escapes were to the Filipino clubs with live bands to rival the best entertainers in any club in new Dubai.

This night was such a night. I decided to venture back to Bur Dubai to visit two Filipino clubs which I frequent and drop by another which I had heard about. As my cab made his way towards **KitaKits**, my first stop for the night, I noticed a temporary outdoor stage had attracted a crowd. I paid my fare, hopped out and discovered an unexpected delight.

Under a banner that read 'Soul of the City', 3 drummers beat on white, plastic buckets, their movements synchronized in groovy rhythms. A crowd of hundreds watched, seated on beanbags, standing in throngs, absorbing the beat.

I was surprised to find that Al Ghurair Centre in Deira has become somewhat 'posh' with its beautiful roundabouts and well-lit sidewalks. Across the street, a Ferris wheel spun, games and arcades lit up brightly.

The drummers interact with the audience members, for whom it is a rare treat to see live performers. The children in attendance are enthralled. Onlookers capture the moments on their cameras and phones. The drummers clap out rhythms for the crowd to clap back. They mock the audience's shy nature. Everyone has a laugh. The drummers clown around and soon the crowd is involved.

The drumming trio starts to bang on storage drums, the kind in which you'd store rainwater. Women in niqab, men with their arms around each other, Western, Eastern, old, young, all gather on the plastic green grass, surrendering to the rhythm. This beat transcends all language. Between sets, the drummers return to engage the audience before turning their attention back to their drumsticks. Next, the trio bangs on the backdrop of hung tin plates behind them, a symphony of tings and clanks. They show us how to do so much with such simple, every day objects. The beat shifts from rock to Indian pop. The crowd erupts in energy.

Google Maps tells me that my destination is only a few blocks away, and I start to make my way to the hotel. This area is one of the very few in which you can get around on foot or on bike. I enjoy the walk, observing the Thursday night commotion around me.

On Al Muteena Street, across from a heavily populated walkway, you will find the **Marco Polo Hotel**. Kitakits is on the side, guarded by a tall, white wall topped with flags.

You will walk through a smoky tunnel of cubic neon lights, and enter the club to find stacked bars and brightly-coloured cocktails, a well-dressed stage and more neon.

A DJ is playing salsa music and three couples are dancing, while others eat their dinner. The bass beats in my chest. A band starts to set up on stage. A buffet lines the back wall and people line up to pile their plates.

On the dance floor, a man holds his woman by the waist; she flourishes in a diva pose. It seems that every couple dancing has studied salsa and merengue, and are determined to incorporate such moves no matter the song.

Then, the lights dim and the opening act begins. The band at Kitakits includes a saxophone player, guitarist, bassist, keyboard player, drummer and two women in silver dresses who croon *Celebrate Good Times* for their first number. One of the singers is 'Naughty' in her plunging neckline, and the other is 'Nice' in a more girly dress, looking quite innocent. Naughty starts to sing *I Will Survive* with super extra reverb on the mic.

All of the couples here are seasoned dancers. I've stepped into a musical. The waitress sings "Peaaanuts ma'am" as she places a bowl in front of me. They are the best peanuts I've ever tasted. Deep fried with garlic. Divine. I see that one man is wearing a shirt that says: *Filipino Dance Club Dubai* and it all makes a bit more sense.

She wears a blue miniskirt and dances with joy, straight, brown hair twirling behind her. He wears a Bruce Lee T-shirt and smiles at her each time their hands meet. Another woman half-dances, half-laughs her way around the small dance floor. She wears a leopard-print dress with a big black bow in the back. One group has ordered a personal Carlsberg tap to their table. 'Nice' starts to sing *September*, while a group of men sitting on a high-top table eye the band and scowl. 'Nice' actually has a decent singing voice. She is warmed up now and is looking more womanly with each swish of her hips.

Two waitresses laugh in the corner of the bar, dancing in their maroon vests. I ask if there is a special Kitakits drink. They bring me a Bullfrog; the 'special' for the ladies.

I eye the menu and discover that it features an array of pork knuckles, or pata[1], which you can have deep fried or grilled. Filipino noodles star on the menu as well.

'Naughty' and 'Nice' slip off stage and soon our hosts for the evening emerge: Rega and Sweet Dexter - the entertainers who I have returned to see. They greet their audience in English, then slip into Tagalog. Then they sing. Sweet Dexter is wearing his signature nerdy glasses, hair combed over, totally diva-licious, while Rega is singing in falsetto. The sax player is totally killing it on this song. Very fabulous.

Leopard print laughs whenever she does anything sexy. There's something endearing about it. The band alternates between feel-good songs and love ballads. They also take requests. Above the band, on a big TV a video plays of a girl accepting a proposal in front of the stage, once upon a time, in Kitakits. I discover

1. A FILIPINO DISH CONSISTING OF COOKED PIG TROTTER OR KNUCKLES SERVED WITH A SOY VINEGAR DIP.

that Kitakits actually means 'See you there!' in Tagalog.

My Bullfrog arrives, bright blue and bitter. The bar is still, well lit and not quite full. Rega and Sweet Dexter announce the sing-along or Karaoke portion of the night, inviting guests to serenade us. A thin, quaint man jumps up to the stage and belts out *I want to lay you down on a bed of roses/ for tonight I sleep on a bed of nails*. The two MCs make jokes between each singer, and are there to support them should they lose tempo or forget lyrics. It's still very early in the evening, and I'm not a heavy drinker, but after two sips of my bullfrog, I croak.

I put in a special request for Rega and Sweet Dexter to sing an Adele song of their choice. A year ago I heard them sing Adele better than the songstress herself, and became an instant fan of the duo. Rega has the voice of a virginal country angel from Midwestern America. Sweet Dexter commences an interpretive gesture dance. I am amused and happy to continue on to my next locale for the evening.

My next destination was the first venue I ever explored in Bur Dubai. Welcome to the **Marine's Club** at the Sea View Hotel. To reach the club you will have to walk to the back of the hotel lobby, head down a grey hall, pass the security room and exit through a rusty, metal door. You will suddenly find yourself in a liminal corridor. Pay your entrance fee, hand over all water bottles and you will be ushered up some dark stairs and into another world.

Walking in, you might think you have found a mini Jamaica, with the dancers in small, tight dresses and the reggae blasting. Past the high-top tables and rush

of the bar, you will find a few intimate tables close to the stage. Peanuts and popcorn are served with cold beers.

I notice that the club has had a bit of a makeover. The decorations are white and blue with bags of sea shells hang on the walls alongside the new circular mirrors. The chairs are new and the place looks cleaner, shinier. The live band is what makes a trip to the Sea View hotel so worth it.

I spot the one I came to see: the goddess of the bass guitar. She has a new tattoo sleeve. Years ago, on my first visit to the venue, the Italian told me that he was in love with her and explained her tragic story: a Filipino mail-order bride, she discovered American classic rock in the United States. Eventually she left her husband and moved to Dubai to join this awesome Filipino-American classic rock cover band. I never verified whether this legend is myth or fact, but I do know that this woman is one of the most enthralling performers I have ever seen. I didn't remember her tattoos or lip piercing, but I quickly recognised her on stage presence, the losing herself in six chords, the long brown hair curled and hanging over her band tee, chains and jeans.

The Golden Star Band begins to play - two guitarists, a bassist, a keyboard player and drummer thrash out *Free Bird*. The guitarist plays the intricate solos so casually, his American eagle belt buckle glistening under the LED lights. He even plays a few chords using his tongue. The goddess wears an ankh around her neck, chews gum, and clearly lives for rock n' roll. She head bangs and slams her guitar, mouth open, revealing a tongue ring. When the Italian introduced me to her, he told me,

quite heartbroken, that after her American husband, the goddess has vowed to never be with another man. I buy it.

Next, the band is joined by four dancers, who have traded in their old wardrobes of colourful sequins for coordinated black tube-tops and boots. Together the group sings an incredible rendition of *Bohemian Rhapsody*.

In a display of musical prowess, the goddess plays the guitar introduction to *Sweet Child of Mine* behind her back. Then she tires of using her hands and holds the frets using her mic stand. She really is incredible to watch. In the next tune, Eric Clapton's *Cocaine*, the goddess plays the drum kit. She slams away, and I don't think that life exists for her outside of this club and these girls, the disco lights and drunken camaraderie; the men who come to forget themselves.

I am tempted to watch her all night, but am very excited to discover the musical offerings of **Ratsky's**, a club I have heard much about, but have never visited. I take a cab to the Karama hotel, and push past a dark blue foyer and into a giant club with multiple disco balls and two dance pits. There is a long stage and on it a guitarist, bassist, drummer and three back-up singers supporting a Filipino reggae star named Dragon, performing a Marley medley.

Dragon's dread locks are so long that I doubt their authenticity. The dancers are all wearing coordinated outfits - blue on top and tight black below. The hundreds of people in the club, from various walks of life, all groove to *All We Need is Love*. Still, the dance pits wait patiently for the first of the brave to step into them.

On the tables in the club you will find

popcorn or platters of fruit. One of the backup singers sings *Unbreak my Heart* and is joined in chorus by a table of young business executives sitting next to me.

I am surprised that this band performs every night. They are pretty decent, but are a mere seven people. Online Ratsky's boasts its fourteen-piece band. Still, the seven provide an entertaining show with choreographed dancing.

Soon the band breaks and the DJ takes over, together with his legion of lasers. The dance floor swells with worker bees escaping into the comfort of the bass. One of the dance pits is dominated by girls, if only for a moment, and instantly, the men

in the club encircle them, the ladies quickly disperse.

I glance around and realize that I can mostly only see men. There is one woman for every three men in Ratsky's, a big difference from the female-dominated Marine's Club, and the couple-friendly Kitakits.

With a smile on my face, I watch a group of Italians lose themselves in the *Harlem Shake*, as the song bleeds into a hip-hop anthem, the men wrap their arms around each other and *jump! jump!*

I observe the one who doesn't jump in time with the group, and smile.

STOLEN NOTES FROM
LITTLE BLACK BOOKS

SHOP

IF YOU GO TO THE **CAMEL MARKET** ON THE AL AIN ROAD YOU CAN BUY A CAMEL BLANKET. IT'S A COARSE BLANKET, LIGHT BLUE AND PATTERNED, WITH A HOLE IN THE MIDDLE FOR THE CAMEL'S HUMP. IT MAKES AN EXCELLENT BEACH MAT AND BECAUSE OF THE HOLE IT ALSO MAKES A GOOD OVERSIZED PONCHO.
IT COSTS ABOUT AED 25.

HOUSE OF PROSE, A SECOND-HAND BOOKSHOP. IN THEORY YOU CAN SELL BOOKS THAT YOU HAVE BOUGHT BACK TO THEM. THERE ARE OLDER BOOKS ABOUT DUBAI, COFFEE TABLE BOOKS THAT SEEMED LIKE A GOOD IDEA IN THE 1980S BUT ARE NOW A RELIC OF TIMES PAST. THERE ARE BACK ISSUES OF NATIONAL GEOGRAPHIC. UPSTAIRS, THERE IS A LOW, DISORDERED ATTIC, WITH BOXES OF UNSORTED BOOKS.
JUMEIRAH PLAZA, JUMEIRAH, DUBAI.
TEL: 04 344 9021

CARTEL IN ALSERKAL AVENUE TO SAMPLE EMERGING REGIONAL FASHION DESIGNERS.
6 ALSERKAL AVENUE, AL QUOZ 1, STREET 17.
TEL: 04 388 4341

HAVE A SENSORY EXPERIENCE IN THE **FARMERS' MARKET** EVERY FRIDAY FROM 9AM – 1PM ON *THE TERRACE, JUMEIRAH EMIRATES TOWERS HOTEL.*

O'DE ROSE STORE SELLS ITEMS FROM THE REGION: BOHEMIAN NECKLACES, CHIC MIRRORS, TEA GLASSES, COFFEE CUPS, EMBELLISHED TUNICS, FUNKY T-SHIRTS AND UNUSUAL FURNITURE.
99, AL WASL ROAD, UMM SUQEIM 2.
TEL: 04 348 7990

FOR EDGY ABBAYAS AND TURBANS TRY **MALAAK** AT *JUMEIRAH TERRACE,*
JUMEIRAH 1.
TEL: 04 386 0570

PETALS AT THE **COURTYARD** IS LIKE AN OTTOMAN PALACE FILLED WITH HAND BLOWN GLASS, VENETIAN MIRRORS, ANTIQUES AND DECORATIVE PIECES REPRODUCED IN ANTIQUE STYLE. LAVISH CHANDELIERS, INTRICATE TABLE WEAR, DRY AND NATURAL FLOWER ARRANGEMENTS AND WROUGHT IRON FURNITURE.
THE COURTYARD OUTLET, STREET # 4B, AL QUOZ INDUSTRIAL AREA 1, DUBAI, BEHIND AL TAYER MOTORS.
TEL: 04 347 3003

GLOBAL VILLAGE IS A GREAT SPRAWLING FAIR THAT SELLS GOODS IN PAVILIONS ARRANGED BY COUNTRY, A GREAT WINTER DESTINATION IN DUBAI WHERE YOU CAN BUY REASONABLY PRICED ITEMS FROM ALL OVER THE WORLD. DON'T LEAVE WITHOUT SOME YEMENI HONEY AND SOME JORDANIAN ZAATAR.
SHEIKH MOHAMMED BIN ZAYED ROAD EXIT 37.
TEL: 04 362 4114

EAT & DRINK

A FINE OUTDOOR LOUNGE IS TO BE FOUND AT THE **101 DINING LOUNGE AND BAR**. *ONE AND ONLY, THE PALM DUBAI (THE PALM WEST CRESCENT). TEL: 04 440 1030*

FISH HOUSE RESTAURANT WHERE THE EMIRATI CHEF PREPARES EXQUISITE SEAFOOD INCLUDING FISH SAYIDENA. *FOOD COURT AREA, UPTOWN MIRDIF, MIRDIF, DUBAI KHANFAROOSH. TEL: 04 288 5548, 055 430 0310*

ASTORIA HOTEL IN BUR DUBAI HAS THE **YAK N YETI**. THOUGHT TO BE A NEPALI RESTAURANT WITH ENTERTAINMENT BUT IT'S MORE OF A NEPALI CLUB WITH FOOD, RIOTOUS MUSIC, SINGING AND DANCING, PACKED WITH NEPALIS. ENJOY MOMOS AND NEPALI DUMPLINGS.

SMILING BKK, A FAVOURED DUBAI INSTITUTION FOR DELICIOUS THAI FOOD IN A BIZARRE, FUN SETTING. TRY THE LEMONGRASS ICED TEA. VISIT THE BRANCH IN *JUMEIRAH, AL WASL PLAZA, AL WASL ROAD, NEAR SAFA PARK. TEL: 04 349 6677*

FOR TRADITIONAL LEBANESE & MIDDLE EASTERN CUISINE, AND A NIGHTLY BELLY DANCING SHOW, CHECK OUT **AL QASR**, ON *JUMEIRAH BEACH ROAD. DUBAI MARINE BEACH RESORT & SPA, JUMEIRAH. TEL 04 346 1111*

PAD THAI IN *SOUK MADINAT JUMEIRAH*, TAKE THE BOAT RIDE IN! AND REMEMBER TO WALK AROUND MADINAT JUMEIRAH. IT IS NOT EXACTLY OFF THE BEATEN PATH IN DUBAI, BUT WORTH A VISIT AT NIGHT FOR THE WATER, LIGHTS AND OUTDOOR OPTIONS.

FOR A DELICIOUS COCKTAIL TRY **LA PETITE MAISON**, *DIFC*.

ATMOSPHERE BAR LOUNGE ON THE 122ND FLOOR, *BURJ KHALIFA TOWER* FOR THE BEST VIEW IN TOWN.

HAVE A CUP OF TEA IN THE VERY FANCY **AL QASR HOTEL** AND ADMIRE THE CHANDELIERS!

BETAWI CAFÉ IN KARAMA, A FAMILY-RUN INDONESIAN RESTAURANT OPERATING OUT OF A HOME. *4B STREET, BEHIND THE MINISTRY OF HEALTH, KARAMA. TEL: 056 759 8118*

RAVI'S IN SATWA IS A LOCAL FAVOURITE FOR PAKISTANI AND INDIAN FOOD. DELICIOUS, QUICK AND WITH NO FRILLS ATTACHED. *AL DHIYAFA RD. TEL: 04 331 5353*

FOR A HEFTY DOSE OF JAPANESE, THAI AND KOREAN DISHES, VISIT **SHOGUN**, AND PACK A LARGE APPETITE. *AL GHURAIR CITY. TEL: 04 228 5568*

SHABASTAN AT THE *RADISSON BLU HOTEL* FOR DIVINE IRANIAN FOOD. *DUBAI DEIRA CREEK, BANIYAS RD. TEL: 04 205 7333*

ALTA BADIA RESTAURANT IN THE *EMIRATES TOWER HOTEL* IS NAMED AFTER A SKI DESTINATION IN NORTHERN ITALY AND OFFERS ITALIAN CUISINE AND FINE DINING. *TEL: 04 319 8771*

CAMEL BURGERS IN BASTAKIYA, ONE OF THE OLDEST RESIDENTIAL AREAS OF DUBAI, AND A HISTORIC SITE. THE CAMEL BURGERS CAN BE FOUND IN *AL FAHIDI STREET.*A TEL: 04 354 0705

NOODLE BOWL IN *SATWA, 2 DECEMBER STREET* IS RUN BY A HONG KONG CHINESE NATIVE NAMED DAVID. SERVES NOODLES IN VARIOUS FORMS AND DIM SUM.

TRADITIONAL EMIRATI FOOD AT THE **SHEIKH MOHAMMED CENTRE FOR CULTURAL UNDERSTANDING**. BREAKFAST IS HOSTED EVERY MONDAY & WEDNESDAY AT 10AM (AED 60 PER PERSON). LUNCH IS HOSTED EVERY SUNDAY & TUESDAY AT 1PM (AED 70 PER PERSON). CULTURAL DINNER EVERY TUESDAY EVENING AT 7PM (AED 95 PER PERSON). CULTURAL BRUNCH EVERY SATURDAY AT 10:30AM (AED 80 PER PERSON). *HOUSE 26, AL MUSSALLAH ROAD, AL FAHIDI DISTRICT, BUR DUBAI.*
TEL: 04 353 6666

LIVE MUSIC DANCING

THERE ARE VARIOUS RUSSIAN CABARET BARS IN DUBAI. THE MEN AND WOMEN DANCE FLAMBOYANTLY TO A SERIES OF SETS WHILE YOU EAT RUSSIAN FOOD. **THE BOLSHOI** IN *THE MOSCOW HOTEL* IN DEIRA IS A FAVOURITE WITH A GREAT DANCE SHOW. THERE IS ALSO **TCHAIKOVSKY** IN THE *BYBLOS HOTEL* IN THE MARINA. DOWNSTAIRS AT THE *BYBLOS HOTEL* IS THE **NELL GWYNNE ENGLISH PUB** WHERE FOUR WOMEN MAKE UP A STRING QUARTET: TWO VIOLINS, A VIOLA AND A CELLO. THEY PLAY CLASSICAL MUSIC, THEN THEY CHANGE TO ELECTRIC INSTRUMENTS AND PLAY COVERS OF ANYTHING FROM THE KILLERS TO LED ZEPPELIN.

ORIGINALLY A MUSICAL SENSATION AND THEATRE VENUE FROM LEBANON BY THE ENTREPRENEURIAL AND ECCENTRIC TALENT MICHEL ELEFTERIADES, **MUSIC HALL**, A CONCERT HALL WITH FOOD, DANCING AND SEVERAL BANDS PERFORMING NIGHTLY, IS NOW A DUBAI HIT. A LITTLE PRICEY, BUT KNOWN FOR ITS EXCELLENT MUSICAL SETS. *JUMEIRAH ZABEEL SARAY.*
TEL: 056 270 8670

JAZZ AT **PIZZA EXPRESS**. WEEKLY EVENTS FROM FLOETRY TO REGGAE TO MUSIC JAM NIGHTS. MORE CASUAL, MUSICAL AND FUNKY THAN YOUR AVERAGE DUBAI MUSICAL JOINT, AND WITH GOOD PIZZA! *NEXT TO MÖVENPICK HOTEL, JUMEIRAH LAKES TOWERS, CLUSTER A.*
TEL: 04 441 6342

MUSIC ROOM FOR LOCAL CONCERTS AND MUSICIANS, POETRY EVENTS AND HIP HOP NIGHTS. A SOLID ALTERNATIVE VENUE TO THE GLITZY NIGHTCLUBS OF DUBAI. DIM LIGHTING, EXCELLENT SOUND SYSTEM AND REASONABLE PRICES. A RELAXED ATMOSPHERE, WITH LITTLE PRETENTIOUSNESS. *MAJESTIC HOTEL, AL MANKHOOL RD.*
TEL: 04 501 2534

LET OFF STEAM

THE ARCHIVE. VISIT THE LIBRARY, HAVE LUNCH, DO YOGA AND CATCH **RIPE**, THE FRIDAY MARKET. *SAFA PARK, GATE 5.*
TEL: 04 349 4033.

THE SHARJAH GOLF & SHOOTING CLUB. THEY DON'T LET YOU TAKE PHOTOS OF PEOPLE YOU DISLIKE TO STICK TO THE TARGETS. BUT THEY DO LET YOU FIRE A MAGNUM LIKE YOU'RE DIRTY HARRY.

ON THE WAY TO THE *BAB AL SHAMS RESORT*, BIKE ENTHUSIASTS WILL DELIGHT TO FIND THE 85KM **DUBAI CYCLING COURSE**, LOCATED ON *AL QUDRA ROAD* AMIDST ROAMING ORYX AND FALCON HUNTERS.

GET THE FALCON'S-EYE VIEW OF DUBAI FROM A **HOT AIR BALLOON** AND WATCH HOW THE SILVER OF THE CITY MELTS AWAY INTO THE GOLD OF THE DESERT. AN ADULT TICKET STARTS AT 995

AED AND PICK UP IS FROM THE *DUBAI DESERT CONSERVATION RESERVE*. GROUP CHARTERED RATES ARE AVAILABLE.

FRIDAY AFTERNOON **KUSHTI**, TRADITIONAL INDIAN WRESTLING IN THE SAND, BEHIND THE *DEIRA FISH MARKET*. IT'S A FORM OF SPORT POPULAR IN INDIA AND PAKISTAN, AND HUNDREDS OF DUBAI'S LABOURERS, TAXI DRIVERS AND FISH MERCHANTS WATCH AND CHEER ON AS MEN IN LOINCLOTHS GRAPPLE WITH EACH OTHER IN THE SAND.

THE MIRACLE GARDEN, THE LARGEST FLOWER GARDEN IN THE WORLD. *AL BARSHA SOUTH*. TEL: 04 422 8902

NEED OUD OIL BLEND AND DUKHOONS? TRY **YAS** PERFUMES AT THE *DUBAI MALL*.

DELICIOUS DATES AND EXCELLENT FOOD FROM **BATEEL**, WHICH ALSO SELLS CHOCOLATE, PASTRIES AND AN INTERNATIONAL MENU. **BATEEL** CAN BE FOUND IN VARIOUS VENUES AROUND THE CITY.
THE MARINA IN UNIT B-5, BELOW AL MESK TOWER, MARINA WALK. TEL: 04 368 4696
FESTIVAL CITY IN SHOP 102, GROUND FLOOR, NORTH OVAL, DUBAI FESTIVAL CITY.
TEL: 04 232 8856

FOR THE BEST MANI-PEDI IN TOWN HEAD TO THE **NAIL SPA** AT *THE MERCATO MALL*.
TEL: 6005 44001

AUTHENTIC TURKISH **HAMMAM** AT *THE JUMEIRAH ZABEEL SARAY, WEST CRESCENT, PALM JUMEIRAH*.
TEL: 04 453 0000

FOR A QUIET STROLL IN THE PARK TRY **AL KHOR PARK**, *MAKTOUM BRIDGE*.
QUIZ NIGHT IN **JEBEL ALI CLUB**. *OLD JEBEL ALI VILLAGE, JEBEL ALI FREE ZONE*.
LANDMARK: NEAR IBN BATTUTA MALL.
TEL: 04 884 6628

FEEL LIKE BEING AIRBORNE AND DEFYING GRAVITY INSIDE A MALL? TRY **IFLY** IN *MIRDIFF CITY CENTER*.
TEL: 04 231 6292

VISIT

THE SHARJAH ART MUSEUM. UPSTAIRS IS THE SHEIKH'S PERSONAL COLLECTION OF ORIENTALIST ART.
TEL: 06 556 6002

JUMEIRAH MOSQUE (DAILY TOURS FROM 10AM).
JUMEIRAH BEACH ROAD. TEL: 04 353 6666

DUBAI MOVING IMAGE MUSEUM IN *TECOM*.
TEL: 04 421 6679, 056 171 1464

BAIT AL BANAT WOMEN'S MUSEUM.
AL SABKHA. TEL: 04 234 2342

BEACHES / BEACH BARS

KITE BEACH IN *UMM SUQEIM*.

SERENE SETTING, LAVISH AND YET COMFORTABLE, AND RIGHT ON THE WATER, **THE JETTY BAR** IS WORTH A VISIT *ONE & ONLY ROYAL MIRAGE HOTEL*.
TEL: 04 399 9999

THE TERRACE AT *PARK HYATT DUBAI* IS A PERFECT VENUE TO UNWIND AND ENJOY THE SUNSET OVER THE WATER.
TEL: 04 317 2222

SUNSET BEACH *JUMEIRAH BEACH ROAD, JUMEIRAH* AT NIGHT TO SEE THE BIOLUMINESCENT WAVES.

CONTRIBUTORS

AMINA ABDEL-HALIM SPENT HALF HER LIFE IN THE US AND THE OTHER HALF IN THE MIDDLE EAST. SHE HAS A DEGREE IN COMMUNICATIONS FROM UC BERKELEY AND A MASTERS DEGREE IN ADVERTISING FROM UT AUSTIN. SHE LIKES COMIC BOOKS AND WAS INTO FOOD BEFORE THE TERM 'FOODIE' EXISTED. SHE CURRENTLY LIVES IN LOS ANGELES WHERE SHE WORKS IN ADVERTISING, WRITES, COOKS AND FREQUENTLY SQUEEZES TOMATOES AT FARMERS' MARKETS.

JALAL ABUTHINA IS AN IRISH/LIBYAN PHOTOGRAPHER AND INDEPENDENT VISUAL ARTIST BASED IN DUBAI SINCE 1992. HIS WORK HAS BEEN EXHIBITED THROUGHOUT THE UAE AS WELL AS INTERNATIONALLY, AND HAS BEEN FEATURED IN NUMEROUS INTERNATIONAL ART AND PHOTOGRAPHY PUBLICATIONS SUCH AS *BEAUTIFUL/DECAY, DAZED AND CONFUSED, DESIGN BOOM, DETNK.COM, CANVAS MIDDLE EAST, CANON MIDDLE EAST, GULF NEWS* AND *CONTEMPORARY PRACTICES*. JALAL CURRENTLY WORKS BETWEEN THE TOURISM AND COMMERCIAL PHOTOGRAPHY WORLD.

DIYA AJIT IS PROUD TO CALL DUBAI HER BIRTHPLACE. A VISUAL ARTIST, FASHION AND MEDIA PERSONALITY, DIYA HAS BEEN DESCRIBED AS A LEADING CREATIVE POLYMATH AND A VISUAL ARTS MAVEN WITH A CAREER SPANNING FILM & TV, ADVERTISING, THE ARTS, FASHION, MEDIA AND PUBLISHING. SHE IS A BRAND AMBASSADOR TO SEVERAL FASHION LABELS AND BOUTIQUES. SINCE 2012 SHE HAS FOCUSED ON A CAREER IN FASHION PUBLISHING AND WAS PART OF THE LAUNCH TEAM OF *STYLE.COM/ARABIA* PRIOR TO HER CURRENT ROLE AT THE GCC'S LEADING ONLINE FASHION MAGAZINE *SAVOIR FLAIR*.

RICHARD ALLENBY PRATT IS A BRITISH PHOTOGRAPHER BASED IN DUBAI SINCE 2000. HE HAS SHOT EDITORIAL FEATURES FOR *THE GUARDIAN, THE NEW YORK TIMES, DER SPIEGEL* AND *TIME MAGAZINE*. HIS ONGOING PROJECT, CONSUMPTION, LOOKS AT THE WAY THAT LANDSCAPES IN THE UAE HAVE BEEN IMPACTED UPON BY THE EXPONENTIAL ECONOMIC GROWTH IN THE REGION. RICHARD IS A REGULAR COLUMNIST AT *GREEN PROPHET*, THE LEADING WEBSITE CONCERNED WITH ISSUES OF SUSTAINABILITY IN THE MIDDLE EAST. HIS HOBBY IS FINDING INEXPLICABLE LANDSCAPES ON *GOOGLE EARTH* AND VISITING THEM TO FIND OUT WHAT THEY ARE.

AUSTYN ALLISON IS A BUSINESS JOURNALIST FROM SCOTLAND BASED IN DUBAI. HE MOVED HERE TO LAUNCH THE GULF NEWS WEEKLY TABLOID *XPRESS*. HE HAS EDITED *COMMUNICATE MAGAZINE* COVERING MEDIA, MARKETING AND ADVERTISING. HE ONCE WORKED AS A CHEESEMONGER.

HAJER ALMOSLEH IS A PALESTINIAN POET AND WANDERER WHO HAS CALLED DUBAI HOME FOR THE PAST SEVEN YEARS. SHE KNOWS SHE WILL LIVE LONG BECAUSE THE OLDER SHE GROWS, THE WISER SHE THINKS SHE HAS BECOME, THE MORE MISTAKES SHE MAKES.

ANOUSHKA ANAND (NOUSH LIKE SPLOOSH) COMBINES A KITCHEN-SINK BREW OF FILM MAKING, SONG WRITING AND VISUAL ART TO LEAD STORYTELLING BACK TO ITS DAYS OF GLORY. SHE RECEIVED HER BFA FROM CONCORDIA UNIVERSITY, MONTREAL AND HAS A BACKGROUND IN THEATRE DESIGN AND FILM ANIMATION. SHE WORKS AS A FREELANCER AND IS WORKING TOWARDS AN MFA IN ANIMATION, AS WELL AS RECORDING HER FIRST ALBUM IN DUBAI.

MOHAMAD BADR WAS BORN IN 1981 IN LEBANON. HE IS THE RECIPIENT OF THE *2011 SHABAB AYYAM PHOTOGRAPHY AWARD* AND THE *LIVE ACHRAFIEH HONORARY AWARD (2011)*. HE IS THE FOUNDER OF THE *LAKUM HAMRA2AKOUM WA LI HAMRA2*, A PHOTOGRAPHY PROJECT IN LEBANON, AND *MOSAIC: ACHRAFIEH INTERNATIONAL PHOTOGRAPHY CONTEST*, LEBANON'S FIRST INTERNATIONAL PHOTOGRAPHY COMPETITION. SELECTED SOLO SHOWS INCLUDE *AYYAM GALLERY* IN BEIRUT (2012).

ELIOT BEER LIVED AND WORKED IN DUBAI FOR EIGHT YEARS. IN HIS TIME THERE HE WROTE ABOUT CABLES, PRINTERS, BAD ADS, AWARD SCAMS AND AIRLINE BAGGAGE POLICIES. HIS HOBBIES INCLUDE BOOKBINDING, AMATEUR TAXIDERMY AND LYING ABOUT HIS HOBBIES.

PAUL CASTLE SPENDS HIS TIME OCCUPIED BY WRITING THINGS THAT ARE OCCASIONALLY READ BY OTHERS, GROWING AN EVER-LONGER BEARD, COOKING FOR THE MISSUS, SIPPING STRONG TEA AND HERDING NOISY CATS.

DANA DAJANI IS A CURLY-HAIRED PALESTINIAN PERFORMANCE ARTIST AND WRITER WHO BELIEVES IN THE RESILIENCE OF THE HUMAN SPIRIT. SHE RECENTLY MOVED TO DUBAI FROM CHICAGO. SHE TELLS STORIES ON PAPER, ON STAGE AND IN FILM. DANA PERFORMS SPOKEN WORD WITH *FLOETICS*, A SMALL BAND OF DREAMERS WHO CREATE MUSICAL INTERLUDES FOR THE NIGHT REVELLERS OF DUBAI. CATS, MUSHROOMS AND AIRPORTS ARE A FEW OF HER FAVOURITE THINGS.

FRANK DULLAGHAN WORKS AS A COMPLIANCE CONSULTANT. HE HOLDS A BLACK BELT IN JUDO AND A BROWN BELT IN KARATE AND WING CHUN. HE CAN DRIVE ON BOTH SIDES OF THE ROAD AND PLAYS THE GUITAR. FRANK HAS WRITTEN TWO COLLECTIONS OF POETRY PUBLISHED BY CINNAMON PRESS IN THE UK.

REEM FALAKNAZ IS A PHOTOGRAPHER AND A FREELANCE TV PRODUCER/DIRECTOR FROM THE UNITED ARAB EMIRATES. SHE COLLECTS VINTAGE ARABIC BOOKS. SHE WORKS WITH FILM PHOTOGRAPHY, AND LIKES THE OLDER STREETS, AND PEOPLE, OF DUBAI.

ROBERT FERRY IS THE CO-FOUNDER AND DIRECTOR OF *LAND ART GENERATOR INITIATIVE* AND STUDIED IMPACT DESIGN. HE IS A SENIOR CONSULTANT AT TURNER & TOWNSEND. HIS PASSION IS DESIGNING BUILDINGS THAT ACHIEVE COMPLETE HARMONY WITH THEIR LOCAL AND GLOBAL ENVIRONMENTS, AND WITH THE PEOPLE THAT USE THEM, SUCH AS POSITIVE-IMPACT BUILDINGS THAT DOUBLE AS RENEWABLE ENERGY POWER-PLANTS FOR THE SURROUNDING CITY, SOME OF WHICH HAVE BEEN FEATURED IN *SUPERLATIVE EMIRATES* (DAAB PUBLISHING) AND *POPULAR SCIENCE MAGAZINE*.

BALAZS GARDI WAS BORN 1975 IN BUDAPEST, HUNGARY. OVER THE PAST DECADE, BALAZS HAS TRAVELLED TO OVER TWENTY COUNTRIES CHRONICLING CONFLICT OVER WATER AND ESTABLISHED *FACING WATER CRISIS*, AN INDEPENDENT WORLDWIDE PHOTOGRAPHIC EXHIBITION ILLUSTRATING BOTH TYPICAL AND EXTRAORDINARY HUMAN STORIES AND THE FAR-REACHING CONSEQUENCES OF THE WATER CRISIS. CURRENTLY BALAZS IS A 2013 INK FELLOW. HE LIVES IN THE US WITH SHOKA JAVADIANGILANI, HIS PHOTOGRAPHER WIFE, AND CAN USUALLY BE FOUND IN AIRPORT LOUNGES AND REMOTE LANDSCAPES.

LAMYA GARGASH IS AN ARTIST REPRESENTED BY THE THIRD LINE GALLERY. SHE GRADUATED FROM THE AMERICAN UNIVERSITY IN SHARJAH WITH A BA IN VISUAL COMMUNICATION AND SHE HOLDS AN MA IN COMMUNICATION DESIGN FROM CENTRAL SAINT MARTINS IN LONDON. SHE WAS THE FIRST FEATURE ARTIST TO REPRESENT THE UAE AT THE VENICE BIENNALE 2008 WITH A PHOTOGRAPHIC BODY OF WORK TITLED *FAMILIAL*. SHE HAS TAKEN PART IN *DUBAI NEXT*, CURATED BY JACK PERSEKIAN & REM KOOLHAAS AT THE VITRA MUSEUM IN WIL AM RHEIN. SHE IS PARTICIPATING IN THE 2014 HOUSTON/TEXAS BIENNALE.

DENISE HOLLOWAY IS A GRADUATE OF THE CONCORDIA UNIVERSITY FILM PROGRAM. SHE HAS BEEN BASED IN THE UAE FOR THE PAST TEN YEARS AND CURRENTLY WORKS IN DEVELOPMENT WITH *VERITAS FILMS* IN DUBAI AND ABU DHABI.

AZIZA IQBAL IS INFLUENCED BY TRADITION AND CHANNELLING THE CONTEMPORARY. AN ARTIST AND DESIGNER SPECIALISING IN GEOMETRY, PATTERNS AND ILLUSTRATION, HER KEY INSPIRATION IS ISLAMIC ART AND SHE USES TRADITIONAL, AS WELL AS DIGITAL, TECHNIQUES TO EXECUTE INTRICATE PATTERNS. SHE THRIVES ON EQUAL QUANTITIES OF CHAOS AND ORDER.

JAMAL IQBAL FIRST MOVED TO DUBAI IN 2008. HIS FIVE YEARS IN THE CITY, THE LONGEST AMONG THE DOZEN OR SO HE HAS CALLED HOME, HAVE MANAGED TO TEMPER THE TEMPER, SOMEWHAT, AS HE MULTI LIVES AS AN ACTOR, POET, COMIC, WRITER AND PERFORMANCE ARTIST.

AGRI ISMAIL IS A WRITER AND A LAWYER. HIS WORK HAS APPEARED IN *THE CHIMURENGA CHRONIC*, *THE OUTPOST* AND *THE WHITE REVIEW*. FOR YEARS HE HAS BEEN TIRELESSLY LOBBYING TO GET NUTELLA INCLUDED IN THE BOTTOM LAYER OF MASLOW'S HIERARCHY OF NEEDS.

LAFI IS A DOCUMENTARY PHOTOGRAPHER AND FILMMAKER. HIS CAREER, SPANNING OVER FIFTEEN YEARS, HAS TAKEN HIM FROM EXOTIC ASSIGNMENT TO TACKLING SENSITIVE ISSUES SUCH AS THE IMPACT OF CULTURAL BEHAVIOUR ON THE MENTALLY ILL IN THE MIDDLE EAST, AND THE MISGUIDED STIGMATIC ATTITUDE TOWARD THE DISABLED.

DANNA LORCH IS AN AMERICAN WRITER AND POET BASED IN DUBAI. IN HER OTHER LIFE SHE DIRECTS HUMANITARIAN NGOS AND HAS SPENT SOME OF HER BEST MOMENTS IN REFUGEE CAMPS AND HOSPITALS. SHE BLOGS ABOUT THE REGION'S ART AND POP CULTURE.

HIND MEZAINA IS A PHOTOGRAPHER BASED IN DUBAI AND A PART OF LOMOGRAPHY, A GLOBAL PHOTOGRAPHY COMMUNITY THAT FOCUSES ON SPONTANEOUS PHOTOGRAPHY USING ANALOG CAMERAS AND A 'DON'T THINK - JUST SHOOT' PHILOSOPHY.

LAYLA MAGHRIBI WAS BORN TO A PALESTINIAN-LIBYAN FATHER AND SYRIAN MOTHER. SHE HAS WORKED FOR *REUTERS NEWS* AS A VIDEO JOURNALIST AND PRODUCER OF SHORT FEATURES IN THE UAE. FROM GOLD-PLATED TEA-LEAVES, SHOES AND FERRARIS TO ENDANGERED COWS AT A DAIRY FARM, LAYLA HAS SEEN BOTH THE WEIRD AND THE WONDERFUL THAT DUBAI HAS TO OFFER. LAYLA IS NOW A WRITER AND PRODUCER FOR *CNN* IN ABU DHABI.

BASILE MOOKERJEE WAS BORN IN PARIS IN 1987, TO AN INDIAN FATHER AND GREEK MOTHER. A PASSIONATE TRAVELLER, HE CONTINUES TO DO SO WITH HIS PHOTOGRAPHIC WORK. AFTER STUDYING GRAPHIC DESIGN IN LONDON AT CENTRAL SAINT MARTINS, HE PURSUED A MASTERS DEGREE IN PHOTOGRAPHY AND ART DIRECTION AT ECAL IN LAUSANNE, SWITZERLAND. HE IS NOW BACK IN PARIS, BUT HOPEFULLY NOT FOR TOO LONG.

FIONA PATTERSON FLED THE UK A FEW YEARS AGO, A RECESSIONARY REFUGEE SHE STILL SUFFERS FROM THRIFT. SHE ENJOYS SEEKING OUT DUBAI'S CULTURAL GREEN SHOOTS.

HUDA SMITSHUIJZEN ABIFARES IS AN AMSTERDAM-BASED TYPOGRAPHER, DESIGNER, WRITER AND THE FOUNDING CREATIVE DIRECTOR OF *THE KHATT FOUNDATION* AND *KHATT BOOKS*. SHE WRITES ON DESIGN AND TYPOGRAPHY IN THE MIDDLE EAST. SHE HAS PUBLISHED BOOKS ON TOPICS SUCH AS ARABIC TYPOGRAPHY (SAQI BOOKS, LONDON. 2001) AND *TYPOGRAPHIC MATCHMAKING IN THE CITY* (KHATT BOOKS, AMSTERDAM 2011). SHE WAS BORN IN BEIRUT, LIVED FOR 8 YEARS IN DUBAI, AND HAS TRAVELLED AND WORKED IN THE MIDDLE EAST SINCE 1994.

ALI TAHERI WAS BORN IN BAHRAIN AND IS OF IRANIAN DESCENT. HE HAS BEEN A RESIDENT OF DUBAI SINCE 2005. HE IS CURRENTLY PURSUING A MASTERS DEGREE IN MEDIA AND COMMUNICATIONS, WHILST WORKING AS A PRODUCER WITH *ANALOG PRODUCTION*. HE IS CURRENTLY WORKING ON A FIRST DOCUMENTARY CONCERNING YEMEN.

JOHN ZADA IS A TRAVEL WRITER AND PHOTOGRAPHER. WHEN HE'S NOT COMPOSING THREE-LINE TELEVISION NEWS HAIKUS (HEADLINES) AT THE CANADIAN BROADCAST CORPORATION TO PAY FOR HIS PIZZA NAPOLETANA HABIT, JOHN CAN USUALLY BE FOUND TRAIPSING AROUND SOME EXTREME QUARTER OF THE PLANET IN A BID (USUALLY SUCCESSFUL) TO ESCAPE HIS FELLOW MAN. THE FORMER DUBAIAN IS CURRENTLY WORKING ON A TRAVELOGUE IN SEARCH OF THE ELUSIVE SASQUATCH IN CANADA'S GREAT BEAR RAINFOREST.

NICK ZAJICEK IS A BRITISH ROVING CAMERAMAN AND PHOTOGRAPHER. BASED IN DUBAI. HE IS CONTINUOUSLY ON THE ROAD RECORDING FACES, LIGHT AND NATURE AROUND THE WORLD. IN WINTER HE WORKS ON CORPORATE FILMS, TV SHOWS, SHORT NARRATIVE STORIES AND PHOTOGRAPHY PROJECTS. IN SUMMER HE TREKS NEW CONTINENTS, READS BOOKS AND LOUNGES ON BOATS.

REWA ZEINATI IS A LEBANESE-AMERICAN POET AND WRITER, SHE IS THE AUTHOR OF THE CREATIVE NONFICTION BOOK ENTITLED, *NIETZSCHE'S CAMEL MUST DIE: AN INVITATION TO SAY 'NO'* (XANADU, 2013), AS WELL AS THE POETRY CHAPBOOK, *BULLETS & ORCHIDS* (CORRUPT PRESS, 2013). ZEINATI IS THE FOUNDER AND EDITOR-IN-CHIEF OF *SUKOON MAGAZINE*, AN ARAB-THEMED, ENGLISH LANGUAGE, ONLINE LITERARY JOURNAL. SHE HAS A MASTER'S DEGREE IN CREATIVE WRITING AND HER WORK HAS BEEN PUBLISHED IN LITERARY JOURNALS AND ANTHOLOGIES WORLDWIDE. SHE WORKS IN ADVERTISING AND LIVES IN DUBAI.

MAJALIS - LAMYA GARGASH